A MURDER OF CROWS
The Story of Penally

A MURDER OF CROWS

The Story of Penally

Margaret Davies

Published by the Author

Copyright © 2001 Margaret Davies

Published in 2001 by
Margaret Davies
Crackwell Farm, Penally, Pembrokeshire
Telephone: (01834) 842031

The right of Margaret Davies to be identified as the Author of the Work
has been asserted by her in accordance with the
Copyright, Designs and Patents Act 1988.

*All rights reserved. No part of this publication may be reproduced, stored in a
retrieval system or transmitted, in any form or by any means without the
prior permission of the publisher, nor be otherwise circulated in any form of
binding or cover other than that in which it is published and without
similar condition being imposed on the subsequent purchaser.*

A CIP catalogue record for this book is
available from the British Library.

ISBN 0 9540428 0 8

Printed and bound in Wales by
Dinefwr Press Ltd.
Rawlings Road, Llandybie
Carmarthenshire, SA18 3YD

To my four 'crow' grandsons

*Tom and Fred born at Palmers Lake
Hector and Hugo born at Crackwell*

Contents

		Page
Foreword		9
Preface		10
Chapter 1	MEDIAEVAL PENALLY	13
	The last witch. Parish Topography.	
	End of the feudal system. Earliest houses. Civil War	
Chapter 2	THE FARMERS DUEL ON PENALLY BRIDGE	53
Chapter 3	GEORGIAN PENALLY	60
	Land enclosure. Gentility. First School. First houses.	
	Agriculture improvement	
Chapter 4	VICTORIAN PENALLY	89
	Education. Religion. Railway. The Army. Characters	
Chapter 5	EDWARDIAN PENALLY	122
	New building. Population. Increase. WW1.	
	Chronicle. Characters	
Chapter 6	1930 TO ELIZABETH II	140
	Modernisation. WW2	
Appendix	LETTERS FROM OLD CROWS	155
	The Hoax. Vicars. Census. Snippets	
Acknowledgements		175

Foreword

I have a window at Crackwell that looks out to a great sweep of the western boundary of the parish. The view can not have altered much in the last 500 years, a few more trees perhaps, and what looks like a toy train passing below occasionally. I realised with a shock that within the last 50 years I have seen many of the farms disappear altogether, and the rest, save one or two, diversify and adapt the use of the land. Newcomers to Penally will find it strange to learn that farming was such an integral part of village life. Farmers are an endangered species now.

It started me wondering how these farms came about and how the village developed, but I could find no book that covered this period. I am not a writer but rather an enthusiastic amateur historian, and what follows is my attempt to fill this gap.

The early history of Penally when it was used as a 'port' in early Christian times is already well documented. The watery nature of the place has played a big part in the history of the parish, and until the Alun river was culverted in the 20th century, and the Ritec which flooded the salt marsh was enclosed, it was a difficult place to reach at high tide. The whole parish remained thinly populated until the end of the 18th century when land enclosure and improved farming methods paved the way for some stability and growth.

It is this growth that I felt needed to be accounted for, before some information is lost forever.

The title of this book is the collective noun for a gathering of crows and seemed appropriate since Penally people have always been called crows. This oddity may be because they are independent, solitary and shy, not unlike the birds. Even today, the true locals prefer to remain unnoticed.

Margaret Davies
Crackwell Farm
Penally

Preface

While this book deals with Penally from medieval times onward, it should not be forgotten that Pen Alun, as it was originally named, has an ancient history, indeed, pre-history.

Old Stone Age hunters found shelter in Hoyle's Cave and Longbury Bank and hunted forests now submerged under Lydstep Bay.

In a midden on Giltar Point was found a fragment of pottery made by the hand of an Early Iron Age potter.

Penally also holds a place of importance as a centre of early Christianity. Its situation near the monastic isle of Caldey and at, or near, one end of the transpeninsular route across Pembrokeshire to Whitesand or Porth Clais so as to avoid the treacherous headlands of western Pembrokeshire, made it familiar to the *peregrini*, or Celtic saints, in their travels between Brittany and Ireland.

In addition, Saint Teilo, whose eminence was such that dedications to him stretch across south Wales in a pattern similar to that of his companion Saint David, was born at *Eccluis Guinnon* (Gumfreston), the church of Wynnio, at or near Penally. When he died, his body was claimed by three places, Llandeilo, where his great monastery was, Llandaff, where he founded a cathedral and, Penally, 'because the burial place of his ancestors was there and he had hereditary rights in the place.' Guonocatui was the abbot of Penally in 706 AD.

Penally was also a place of legend. Noah, son of Arthur, king of Dyfed from 586 to 616, gave land at Pen Alun to St Dyfrig, who spent the greater part of Lent on Caldey. In the Life of Saint Oudoceus, a nephew of Saint Teilo, it is stated that Pen Alun belonged to Saint Dyfrig 'since the time of king Noah son of Arthur.' Pen Alun may have been named after Alun Dyfed, a traditional hero of Dyfed, whose sons appear in The Mabinogion and whose fort, Caer Alun, was said to have been at Haverfordwest.

The thirteenth century Norman church was built on the site of a Celtic church, possibly a Teilo foundation. It has squint passages, a Norman font and a vaulted ceiling. In the south transept lies the tomb of William de Naunton and his wife, Ismay (1260-90).

In the south transept also, stands the tenth century Penally Cross, six foot tall. It has a pierced wheel-head and is decorated overall. It is similar to the Carew and Nevern Crosses except that it is sculpted from a single massive stone, and it is not as tall. It also differs in that, in addition to the characteristically Celtic interlacing spirals and plaited patterns, it has a vine scroll motif in the tradition of Northumbrian art.

There is also the broken shaft of a slab-cross, decorated with beasts and acanthus and other motifs of a similar derivation, and fragments of another. Yet another, now lost, bore an incomplete Latin inscription that proclaimed that it was the cross 'which Mail Domnac erected'.

The presence of so many crosses on this one site indicates the continuing importance of Penally as a Christian centre.

The author, with diligent research, has placed on record the history of Penally from this time forward,

Dillwyn Miles

Chapter 1

Mediaeval Penally

Penally parish would have appeared a barren place in mediaeval times without any boundary hedges. Windswept, it stood out like a headland when it was surrounded by water at different states of the tide, as can be seen in Langley's map below. Much of the land was either scrub, marsh or furze.

Salt laden winds kept any growth low, though thickets of trees grew on the northern slope of the Ridgeway and the inlets along the river Ritec which sprang at St Florence.

There were few people, and the lowliest of them lived a miserable existence.

Nothing was wasted: the furze, or gorse, was a vital fuel, and it also fed and sheltered livestock. In the valley, on the seaward side of the Ridgeway, the sluggish Alun stream would have made a water meadow of the land in front of Court Farm at high tides.

This stream which is fed from Norchard, and by other springs, turned north at Court Farm and spilled into the Ritec. It was not until the 20th century that it was discharged east through a culvert under the burrows to the beach at Giltar. A causeway connected the parish to Tenby, but that, too, would have flooded twice a day.

Any journey was difficult; tracks made by animals, humans, or carts, passed for roads. The only road shown on early maps was the Ridgeway. A sheep walk along the cliff to Lydstep was in use and a lane from Holloway ran alongside the Alun to Lydstep, but would have been impassable at different tides.

The parish was one of the most mystical, a natural home for hobgoblins and the like.

We cannot know what filled the mind of the ordinary man in those days, but through the writings of historians we can guess the uneducated peasant leaned heavily on storytelling and superstition.

In 1534, Henry VIII managed to suppress 8,000 monastic houses and transfer their property to the Crown. This sweeping Dissolution included the group of eight nuns and their prioress, whose Order had held St Deinol's Chapel in Penally since 1301.

Whether it was propaganda or not, it was suggested that many monasteries were in need of cleansing. There had been strong resentment that 'greedy monks gorged their carcass to the point of bursting' and 'who is she that will set her hands to work to get 3d a day and may have at least 20d a day to sleep an hour with a friar, monk, or priest.'[1]

In the summer of 1581 Thomas Cromwell, as vicar general of the king, commissioned a report on all religious houses in the country. The report was known as the Black Book, which Queen Mary later ordered to be destroyed, but enough remains to prove that in the interests of morality, dissolution of the monasteries was absolutely necessary.

One eminent historian says . . . 'If I am to relate the suppression of the monasteries I should relate also why they were suppressed. If I were to tell the truth I should have to warn all modest eyes to close the book and read no further.' Parliament having decreed that all religious houses under the number of twelve in congregation were to be utterly suppressed, and every monastery in Pembrokeshire qualified. The switch from Catholicism to Protestantism in this country was never popular, and Pembrokeshire people were slow to accept it. Remote parishes like Penally did not embrace the new order without some resistance.

Our Vicar in 1600 was Harry Riley who probably did not abandon the Latin Mass entirely, but the new religion was being more strictly enforced, and as late as 1624 when Francis Hudson was our Vicar he was condemned

---

1. Simon Fish, *The Supplication of the Beggars.*

for being a pluralist; that is to say, he still carried on with much of the Catholic form of worship.

It is probably the time when St Teilo's, as it was then, lost its mediaeval wall paintings and popish images.

Peasants, by the author.

In the period up to 1600 there was no village, and the farmers lived either in St Florence or Manorbier. Very little land was enclosed.

Agriculture was the sole employer, and the labourer and his family would have lived in rude outbuildings. Working long hours in all weather and on a poor diet, life expectancy was very short.

Fearing fines, these simple people would attend church, standing at the back, not understanding a word, but eagerly embracing the protective rites of the Mass to ward off evil spirits. They took great comfort from exorcisms, relics, the sprinkling of holy water and particularly in making the sign of the cross.

They believed Churching for women to be a charm to prevent witchcraft, and they resisted change.

At the same time, in the rest of the country, and all over Western Europe, a ferocious witch craze was taking hold. There were many in Pembrokeshire that were considered to have unnatural powers, able to charm warts and cast spells, and there was a great fear of them, but accusations were very rare.

Mathew Hopkins, the 'Witchfinder General' had many zealous followers keen to copy his cruel methods. The country was stirred up to fever pitch and anyone that was wrinkled, female, or kept a black cat, was suspect. Here was a chance to make unjust accusations where there was petty jealousy and antagonism. Spoiled butter or cheese, accidents to property, or the death of livestock were reason enough to find a scapegoat. Wales was better knit socially than Scotland or England and small communities had a tradition of self-help and good neighbourliness. Traditionally, Courts were far more benign in Pembrokeshire, in spite of widespread belief, trials were very few in Wales, and extreme punishment was avoided if possible.

The only witch to be prosecuted in this County was in 1607. According to the account, she was employed at Gumfreston, and I believe she was a daughter of the Lewis family of Penally, who later lived at Carswell.

A Murder of Crows – The Story of Penally

Matthew Hopkins, the self-styled 'Witchfinder General', who was himself hanged in 1647. He went about the country offering his services and extracting confessions by sticking pins into suspects and making them walk until their feet blistered. Two of his victims are here depicted with him. The one on the left is Elizabeth Clark, a one-legged beggar-woman, who gave the names of three of her imps as Holt, Jarmara, and Soake and Sugar. The other confessed that her imps were called Ilemanzar, Pyewackett, Pecke in the Crowne, and Griezell Greedigutt, names, said Hopkins, which 'no mortal could invent'.

The account below, from 'Gwrached Cymru' (Witches in Wales) by Eirlys Gruffydd reads:

'A very interesting prosecution occurred . . .

A Grand Jury presented that Katherine Lewis of Gumfreston, Spinster, otherwise known as Katherine Bowen, wife of Thomas Bowen the yeoman of Tenby by the instigation of the Devil performed diabolical acts of witchcraft, inchantments, charmes and sorceries at Gumfreston on June 27th in that year, by reason of which Richard Brownynge suffered great loss in his goods and chattels

Unfortunately only the presentment exists and we know nothing of the fate of the unlucky lady.'

This is the only indictment for witchcraft in Pembrokeshire which has come to the writer's notice and it is interesting to note that the sole case on record occurred in the South of the County and close to the district in which charming still prevails. If Katherine Bowen had been convicted under the indictment, she would in the event of it being her first offence, have been sentenced under second degree, as her alleged operations had been to injure cattle and goods and not persons. She received one year in prison.

With the Toleration Act of 1689, there was religious freedom for all, and the end of persecution and bigotry.

Welsh gentry were by this time dabbling in rational and scientific thought, but superstition and sorcery belief took longer to disappear in uneducated rural folk. Some would say it is with us still.

It is interesting to find the Courts reluctant to give out death penalties in Pembrokeshire at this time, it seems sorcery did not rate highly on their list of offences, yet punishment was extremely harsh in cases of, for example, theft or slander.

Whipping was generally reserved for children under twelve, and each village had a whipping post. The stocks, in Tenby, and the ducking stool at the harbour, were well used; judging by the cost of constant repairs paid out by the bailiff in records of 1684.

In fact, in the memory of T. W. Hordley, the stocks, which stood at the Five Arches, were used into the late 19th century.

At a spot where the Wheelabout Inn stood on the Ridgeway, it is said that a gibbet hung from a large tree nearby, and that its unfortunate occupants were left there in chains so that they would serve as a warning to other wrongdoers. It could easily be seen from the sea, and wreckers and pirates were often in operation in the area. These practices were considered very serious crimes.[2]

The mediaeval manor of Manorbier comprised the two parishes of Manorbier and Penally held by the De Barri family. The boundary between the two was a line from Tarr Farm past Palmers Lake, over the Ridgeway taking in the two cottages and skirting Norchard continued down to Lydstep.

The whole barony was ruled by a feudal system tightly controlled by the Manorial Courts. The rolling landscape had neither hedges nor walls so that tenant farmers, who often held scattered parcels of land, used their young people as herdsmen or shepherds. There were constant disputes over cattle straying from one tenancy to another, which were dealt with at the Court Baron along with other misdemeanours. There were no farmhouses as such, and the farmer dwelt in neighbouring villages.

A few large houses did exist however, but they were mostly occupied by wealthy merchants from Tenby.

Muster Roll of 1539 for Penaleye
4 men with armour (jackets, etc.)
5 men all nakyd without deffencealle with a staff

This valuable roll was designed to calculate the number of men between 16 and 60 that the King could call upon in defence of the country.

In 1599, George Owen of Henllys estimated that there were 63 people living in the whole parish. A Manorial survey made in 1609 records that Penally had 4 substantial farms, 7 houses and 3 cottages.

The boundary map on page 17 also shows the high Ridgeway and the water would have followed the low contour line all around.

---

2. Ref: Sue Baldwin, Tenby Museum.

Mediaeval Penally

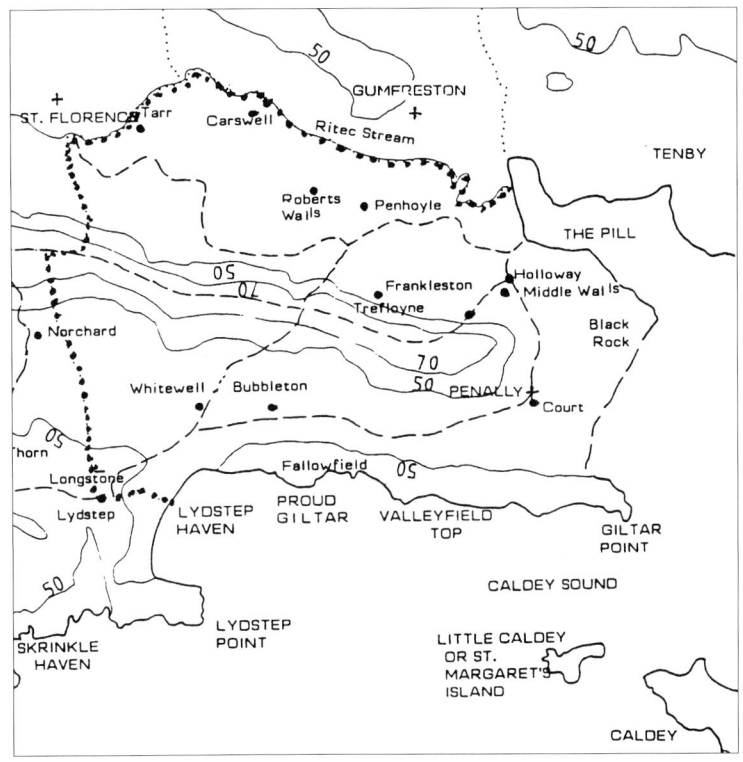

Map showing parish boundary.

The buildings of size that we know existed at that time, other than the Court Leet, the Church and St Deinol were: Trellwyn (1320), La Torre (1324), Carswill (1348), Palmereslake (1326), Whitwill (1326), Hollway and Loudeshope.

The dates only indicate the first time of recording these properties, but they, and many humbler dwellings could have been much older.

They each had rude buildings about them for their workers and families, which made these properties small hamlets in themselves

The manor was sold, and then passed in a series of outright gifts, from one noble family to another, until, finally it was in the gift of Queen Elizabeth to lease the manor to Thomas Bowen Esq., of Trefloyne on

Christmas Eve 1601. This is an important date because it meant that a survey was necessary, and this was taken the same year.

So we get our first insight into the tenants in the parish. Some will be seen to be ancestors of families that were still in the area hundreds of years later. Names like Rowe, Cooke, Voyle, Meyrick, Gwyther, Hillinge, Waters, Millard and Bowen for example.

The reader will have some idea of the feudal system that affected everyone at this time, which was designed by the gentry to protect the gentry, and the Manorial Courts governed all. The surveys will show who leased what, but they will not tell us which of those tenants actually dwelt in the parish.

These records from the court rolls were not always accurate or complete. The following extracts from the survey of 1601, 1609 and 1618 will no doubt interest the parish farmers of today. There were three different types of tenure, briefly explained before each survey.[3]

Freeholders held land by knights' service and attended court separately at 'Longstone', thought to be on the border between Penally and Manorbier, and possibly at what is now known as the 'palace' ruin at Lydstep, a conveniently central meeting place.

They paid one penny farthing the acre and modest rents at Michaelmas. They also paid 3d for non-attendance. There were 18 freeholders in Penally in 1601.

Tenants	Location	Holding	Rent
Walt: Rees Esq 1601	Lydstep	1 mess. 70a. land	1/-
Walter Rice kt 1609		late Griffith Rees	
Thos: Button kt 1618			
Thos. Bowen Esq 1601/9	Trefloyne	2 mess. 80a. land	5/-
Chas:Bowen Esq 1618	Frankleston	1 mess 3a. lateT. Morris	3/4d
	Middle Walls	1 mess. 2a. of Tenby	3/4d
John Thomas 1601	Whitewell	1 mess. 5oxl.	5d
David Meredith			
Owen Thomas 1609			

3. R. F. Walker, *Trefloyne Rentals,* N.L.W. Journal, Vol. XXIX, 1995.

Tenants	Location	Holding	Rent
John ap Owen & John Thomas			
Davie Meredith 1618			
MorganVoyle 1601-18	Holloway	1 mess.	5d
		2 mess. late Sir Jas. Wms	8d
		1mess. late J. Barlow	2d
	Frankleston	2 mess.	4d
John Nicholl 1601	Penholloway	1 mess. 10a.	1/-
David Nicholl 1609	Tarr	1 mess. 70a.	2/-
Chas: Bowen Esq 1618	Lydstep	1mess. 50a.	a rose
Chas: Bowen Esq 1618	Penholloway	1 mess. 20a. late J. Eynon	1/-
Thos: Powell gent 1601-9	Whitewell	½ of 2 mess.	10d
	Lydstep	1mess.	10d
Wm Barlow 1618	Lydstep	1mess. 5oxl.	6d

No details are given for the holdings of John Powell, John Rowe, and Richard Browne, listed free tenants in 1601.

The **husbandry-hold** tenant paid a fixed rent twice a year, and his tenancy could be inherited, he also gave a hen at Christmas for each messuage. Suit to the manor was paid every fortnight and would include labour or carriage services. When a tenant died, a heriot of the best beast was due to the lord.

1601	1609	1618	Rent
Ed: Keathen 9a past:	Ed Keathen	David Palmer	£1/5/8
Joan Trewent 1oxl ar	Joan Trewent	John Millard	18/6
Thos Howell 2oxl ar	Thos Howell	John Howell	18/0
John Millard 2oxl ar	J. Millard 12	John Millard	18/0
Philp.Cooke	P. Cooke 12a ar	David Cooke	£1/7/6
John.Nicholl 8oxl	J. Nycholas	J. Nicholas	3/4
Gelly Meyricke 1a ar	G. Meyricke	Gelly Meyrick Esq	3/4
John Nicholl 8oxl ar	Jane Luney widow	G. Hawkwell 72a ar	£2/6/8
Chas: Julian 11oxl ar	C. Julian 72a ar/cl	C. Jealian	£3/17/8
Edmund Trewent 48a	E. Trewent 38a	Wm Hillinge 60a	£1/13/0

21

And finally the last kind of tenant held land for one life and would receive a copy of court roll as his title deed, for which he was charged 6/8d.

Censory-hold in Penally

1601	1609	1618	Rent
Thos Bowen gent; (under demesnes) Court House 6a mead 30a pasture 44a corse & Penally Park 6a mead 1a corse	Thos Bowen esq Court Ho & bldgs) 6a mead. 30a past 44a corse burrow & burrow Penally park 6a mead 1a corse	Thos Bowen jnr as before 6a mead. 30a ar a sandy burrow 7a Sedge Penally park 6a	£4/1/2
Thos Welsh (Tenby) F.£10 1mess Fallowfield 60a ar	Thos Welshe F.£10 1mess 20a ar 2a corse/mead 38a f/h/c house, barn, stable	Thos Bowen jnr 1mess Vallowfield 20a ar 2a mead 2a corse/30a burrs 10a cliff house, gdn, barn, st cowh. cath, haggard	£3/0/0
Henry Philip F.£10 1 oxl. Ar 1oxl. 4a ar	David Bull, late H. Philp F. 10/- 8a f/h	David Bull 2a ar 2a moory 8a f/h/r	4/0
Thos: Rickard F 6/8	Thos Rickard F. 6/8 cott. ½ land	Thos Rickard	1/8

The Manor had great difficulty in finding good tenants:

'glad was the landlord to hitt on a good thriftie and husbandlie tenant'

but those same good tenants found that they had a firm foot on the first rung of the social ladder. This had always been traditionally reserved for

22

the clergy, but now we see the rise of successful lawyers, medical men, wealthy merchants and yeomen, who were to be gradually absorbed into the landed gentry.

The Bowen family of Trefloyne, were in control for only 43 years until the Civil War of 1644, like all Lords of the Manor they enjoyed the benefits of custom and heriot as well as rents.

In addition to their rents and occasional heriot (having to give their best beast in the event of the tenant's death) lease holders had to render poultry to the lord at Christmas or pay the cash equivalent, for example:

Trefloyne 8 fat geese or 8s
Great Tarr 7 capons or 3s 6d
Court House and Fallowfield 60 rabbits and 4 hens or £1.4.6

also . . . Tarr had to plant 4 oak and 6 ash every year
Trefloyne a dozen of both,
Palmerslake 6 oak, 6 ash and 6 elm
Lydstep double that number of each.

These customs were harsh when one considers that for £1 in 1600 the Bank of England would give £106.50 in 1995 according to the RPI.

Rents and custom were decided at the Court Baron, which was held fortnightly at Lydstep (thought to be in the 'Palace' ruin). Misdemeanors were dealt with at the Court Leet, which was held twice a year at Easter and Michaelmas at Penally, where Court Farm stands today. In the 17th Century, a Customary Court was held at Bubbleton.

Tenants had a rough deal, for as well as paying rent, they were obliged to clean out ditches and repair hedges, to use the Mills the lord dictated, gather his harvest, and contribute cartloads of manure, but they were allowed to quarry limestone on their lands for their own use.

One of the Mills they were obliged to use can be found at the edge of the village of St Florence on the lower road to Penally where it crosses the river Ritec.

You can see the preserved remains of it today. Old documents show that it was a thatched, overshot water mill used to grind corn. It remained important to the community till the mid 19th century when cheap imports of grain saw it converted to a dwelling. It was held by Thomas Bowen in 1609 at a rent of 26/10d.

Drawing by Fanny Price Gwynne of Old Mill, formerly standing near St Florence village.

Penally Mill, referred to in the Hearth Tax of 1670, which Evan Williams occupied, is thought to have been on Penholloway Farm, now Penhoyle. Field names of Big Mill Hill and East Mill Hill indicate that it was on a spur of high land to the east of the farmhouse. It was unlikely that it was ever very efficient, or in use for any length of time, as the Ritec waters there would have been too sluggish, it was unused after 1772.

Did windmills replace these water mills?

Socially, the people of the parish divided into two groups, those with land, or position, and those who were entirely dependent on them.

There was no understanding of hygiene. Plagues, smallpox, and the sweating sickness kept population low at both levels of society. Generally, people were rough in manner, bawdy in speech, and lawless.

The Muster Roll of 1613 showed the following men of arms:

John Bowen of Trefloyne.
Charles Julian of Fallowfield (Clifftop)
Edward Kethin
Thomas Rowe and Benjamin Saunders

At this time farming was in a poor state, through bad husbandry. Crops were meagre, so that those with land tried to improve their income by renting more land. Gradually the system of 'customary-hold' and 'husbandry-hold' fell into disuse and became 'copyhold', which was a more attractive lease, thus creating a lively market for this land.

The more enterprising tenants increased their holdings in this way into substantial farms, which they now found it worth enclosing.

By 1690 there were 38 closed areas of land in all Manorbier and Penally, this was to grow to 700 enclosures by the 19th century.

Houses were built where the farmer worked, so it follows that most of the farmhouses we now know have foundations in the 18th century.

Coastal conditions at this time, meant that a lot of land in the parish was unavailable, and dependent on the state of the tides. The Ritec river, as you can see on the next early sea chart (page 26), was a huge tidal estuary, covering where the Burrows, Golf Club, Marshes and Bridge now lie. Note the great sand banks.

The plan appears in *Plans and Harbours, Bars, Bays and Roads in St George's Channel* by Lewis Morris, published in 1748. Morris had been commissioned by the Board of the Admiralty to carry out a survey of the coasts of Wales in 1737 for the benefit of navigators.

I saw this original chart in the early map exhibition at the Sutherland Gallery at Picton Castle. Note: Tenby was entirely contained within the castle walls.

At this time, a 300-ton barque could sail on the tide beyond East Tarr. This may be hard to imagine, but 'quayside remains were found below Gumfreston Church at St Florence, and at Old Quay.'

The sort of goods imported then included 'spices, olives, lemons, oranges,

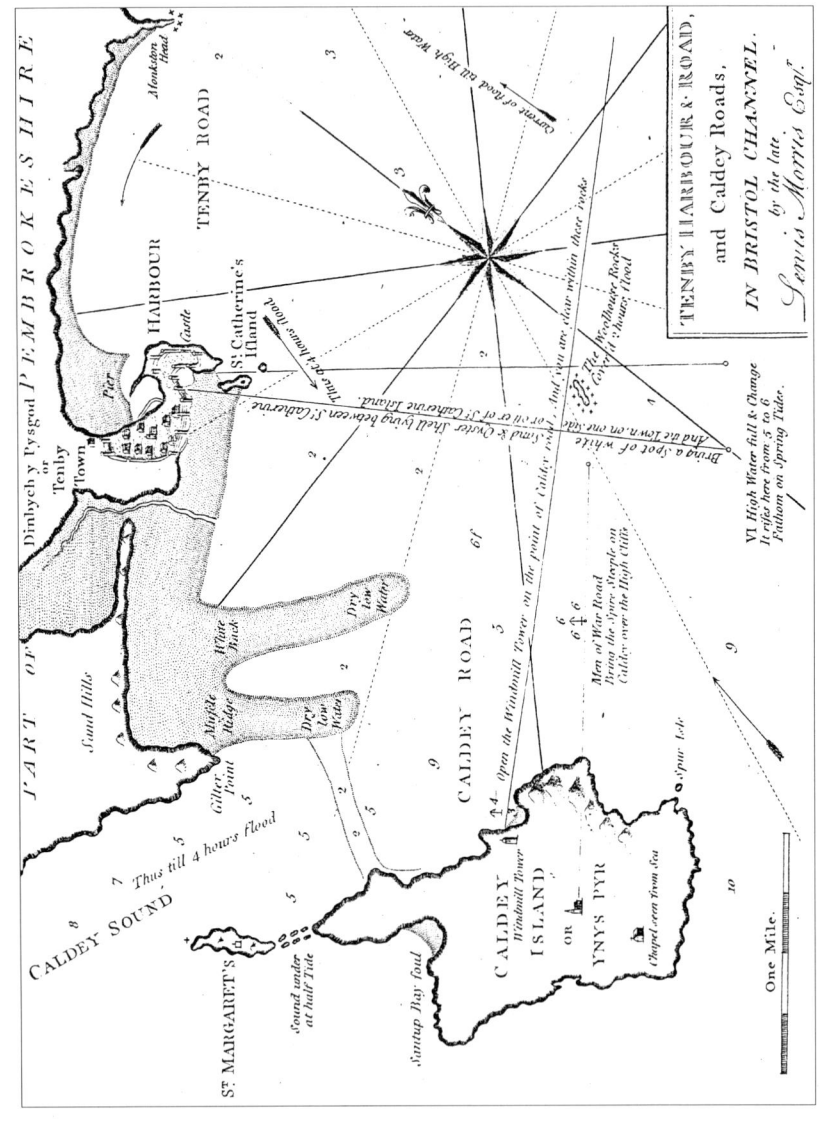

wine, iron bars, salt, pickled-herring, timber tanned skins, gunpowder, silk, and 30 kinds of cloth.'

A view across to Tenby by Charles Norris (abt. 1810).

I think it is likely that those farms near the river inlets would have seen some trafficking in smuggled goods as well as legitimate trade. The lane alongside the church at Gumfreston is known as Howlers Lane, and as a Customs man was called a howler, there must have been good reason for his frequent visits. Incidentally, the last duel in the county was in 1839 and was fought opposite Howlers Lane.

The remarkable cavern known as Hoyles Mouth, although now perhaps 100ft. above high water mark, as well as the numerous glens running into the vale of St Florence, appear to have been formed by the action of the sea:[4]

> *while at a distance of nearly two miles from the latter, at the Causeway Mill, samphire still grows. Nowhere else in the country does it grow so far from the sea.*

---

4. Fanny Price Gwynne, *Tales and Traditions of Tenby.*

The Alun stream too, carried boats as far as what we now know as Penally Railway Station. The inroads of the sea were a cause for concern in 1618.

In August that year, a very detailed survey of the Manor was commissioned by the council of Charles, Prince of Wales. Two commissioners duly reported the findings of a jury of 18 local men, all tenants of the Manor.[5]

What they had to say was decidedly disturbing. Two estates in Penally were particularly threatened by the sea, Fallowfield and Court House, both later combined in Penally Court Farm. Fallowfield – the name survives in the form Valleyfield Top, a high point between Giltar and Proud Giltar – contained 64 acres, of which much was of very little agricultural value: "2 acres of 'corse ground', 30 acres of burrows, sandy ground and sedges and 10 acres of 'ffurze, rocks and cliffe ground'. But these were what did belong unto this Tenement before yt was consumed with the Seas." All the burrows had been lost "as they doe finde by the land Markes there yet remayning. And it was theretofore called by the name of the Newe Marshe when yt was there to be seen." This part of Fallowfield must have lain North of Giltar headland. The Court House estate had suffered even more:

"The sea hath overcome the lowe land and the Burrows of the said Courthouse of Pennally to the number of 60 acres or thereabouts viz; from a certen place there whereon an old Eldern tree did growe neere unto the place called the poynt of Gilter, and from thence the land is quite consumed unto a place called the Pill lake, And right over against a place there called the blacke hall and soe there remayneth but a smale quantitie of Burrow land belonging to that mesuage.

And that the Sea is come within 40 paces unto the lower finne land of the said Messuage and lowe meadowes thereof and is very like in fewe yeares to overcome and drowne the low grounde and soe run into the finne land to the quantitie of a myle in length or thereabouts."

---

5. R. F. Walker, *Coast Erosion at Penally in the 17th Century*. Articles in *Tenby Observer*.

Dr Walker thinks the jurors fears were perhaps exaggerated, but he goes on to say:

"No doubt the battle with the sea has swung to and fro over the centuries, but there are real fears for the future. A high tide can cut a sheer face six or eight feet high into the dunes. If such a tide driven by an easterly gale were to breach the defences on the line of the culvert there would be little to halt its onrush and the sea might well 'overcome and drowne the lowe grounds' perhaps as far as the railway. We know that land on the seaward side of the dunes and burrows was farmed."

There are clear indications of medieval strip cultivation, which showed up in the snowfall of 1961-2 in a small area by Penally by-pass and south of Railway Cottage. On the 7th fairway of Tenby golf course, the grass lies in very shallow, but regular, ridges barely nine feet wide. Over time, with constant wind blown sand, they have been lost in the burrows and marsh, but these small remnants, with no other explanation, would seem to confirm medieval open field cultivation.

Until the time of Elizabeth, the ports and seaways could be compared to the motorways of today; it was nothing to see a hundred head of sail in any harbour. Tenby was one of the busiest ports in the Severn Sea, bursting with vessels of all description and voices shouting in 'Lingua Franca' as well as Devon and Somerset accents.

Merchants and Master Mariners were considered amongst the most important of men, and they lived in style.

The truly splendid houses that used to be in Tenby and Penally were a testament to their wealth.[6]

We imported raisins, oranges, Bay salt and wine from La Rochelle, and exported butter and corn, but during the years of the Spanish Armada, it was forbidden to trade and La Rochelle was under siege.

With trade confined to Channel ports only, the effect was a sharp decline in the wealth of the area and the last of the rich Merchant.

The Civil War, and the plague of 1650 that followed, all but finished

---

6. See Norris's drawings at Tenby Museum.

Another Norris showing Marsh Farm at edge of Tenby.

Tenby. Over 100 of the inhabitants, including 25 children were recorded as victims. There is no record that the plague crossed over to Penally so perhaps its water isolation was after all a blessing. By now Tenby was in ruins, and previously rich merchants like White, Rhys, Pritchard, Bull and Lewis who lived in Penally had departed.

The great lagoon, or PILL as it was known, which separated Penally from Tenby caused Cromwell's army a problem.

They were intent on bombarding Trefloyne and ousting suspected Royalists. But the water was wide enough to frustrate the Roundheads from discharging their cannon at the mansion.

A Parliament print of the day said 'They were obliged to draw nearer to the Earl of

Trefloyne pictured here surrendered to Cornwall's forces in 1644.

Carbery's headquarters; the house being besieged and growing desperate of relief, and after some battery of it, and forcing an outhouse, was delivered on quarter of life and liberty; there was found there forty good horse ready saddled and bridled, and one hundred and fifty men.'

This marked the end of the Bowen family at Trefloyne

After the Civil War, landowners had become stronger, with judicious marriages, or straight land grabbing, they had consolidated their wealth and began to live a grander social life.

At the end of the 17th century, inflation had multiplied four-fold as the following list of rentals indicate.

1692-1726 . . . Trefloyne Rentals

£28 West Tarr	Robert Smith, then Lewis Waters, then Wm Evans.
£30 East Tarr	David Williams, then his widow, then Nicholas Dunn.
£15 Palmerslsake	Stephen Rowe, then Thos Nicholas the widow Abra.
£24 Roberts Walls	Widow Marchant, then Thos Waters, then his widow.
£10 Penholloway/mill	Evan William, then widow Elizabeth and her new husband David Morris, then Wm Rowe +£4.10 mill.
£70 Trefloyne/Marsh	John Philipps, then Wm Phelps, wife Margaret.
£2.10 Middlewalls	John Hughes.
£19 Bubbleton	Peter Nicholas, then Richard Evans.
£12 Drussleton	John Williams, then J. Grant, then J. Thomas (mason).
£10 6 Court + Fallowfield	John Philipps then his son, then Thos Rowe.
£12.10 Lydstep	Widow Taylor.
£1.12 St Margarets	Humphrey Ray of Tenby, then Thos Wiliams ships carpenter with other Tenby property.

A growing number of good yeomen farmers who had extended their holdings, needed to make a living from their land, and they sought to improve their farming methods. Fortunately, they learned crop rotation and discovered a new manure in burnt limestone. This is simply stated, but it was the beginning of an agricultural revolution!

Limekilns sprang up everywhere. Harvests improved, and a surplus of stock and crops were produced.

Droving also became central to the local economy with a greater demand for Welsh cattle in the growing populations of South Wales. The iron industry in Neath, copper smelting in Swansea, and coal mines to feed these new industries, provided the population for a ready market. 20,000 cattle a year were thought to leave Pembrokeshire for the English market through Herefordshire.

Drovers in particular, became wealthy men, and increased wool and dairy produce was exported through the port of Tenby.

The rural population became used to handling money. There was a fresh outlook and confidence in the air, and this new found prosperity was widespread. Sanitation and clean water were seen to be important, the bad old days had passed.

Conditions were right at last, for children to survive and the local population to increase.

By mid 18th Century a hamlet started to grow about the church and the parish had a centre.

Richard Fenton, in his *Historical Tour through Pembrokeshire* claimed that before this time, it would have been beyond the means of most people, to own their own house. Quote:

> 'The countryside between Lydstep and Tenby was formerly thickly studded with houses above the rank of such as farmers might have been supposed to inhabit. Most of them surrounded with a court entered by an arched gateway, and many built on arches.'

The only dwellings we can be sure of were listed in the wonderful records of the 1670 Hearth Tax. These are the earliest records we have on the size of a house which can be gauged by the number of fireplaces it contained, since each hearth was taxed, it shows the wealth of the family. Next are listed 22 properties, nine of which have two or more hearths, so they would have been substantial houses, but which were they?

Hearth Tax for Penaleye 1670

John Thomas	1	Thomas Powell	3
William Lewis	3	Rowland Bull	2
Thomas Waters	2	Rowland Wilkin	1
Thomas Prickard	2	Thomas Lloyd	1
Thomas Rowe	2	Francis Jones(miller)	1
Katherine Phillip	1	John Barsie	1
Humphrey Reed	1	John James	1
Evan Williams, man + Mill		Thomas Lewis	2
Charles Millard	1	Thos: Bowen Esq	8
Henry Jenkins	1	Richard Rowe	1
Jennett Cooke	1	Ethelred Wogan	2

The last name on the list of Ethelred Wogan, was the Vicar of Penally and Gumfreston, who lived in a sizeable house. Could this have been the rectory, described as a dignified mansion by Richard Fenton in his book *Tour through Pembrokeshire*? A large chimney still stands near the present Abbey building, used as an archway to the garden, and with the chimney at the 'St Deinol ruins' on the same land, he would have held 2 hearths.

Frances Hudson, the Vicar for Penally, was dismissed in 1650 for being a pluralist, and it is likely that the Reverend Wogan took his place and cared for the spiritual needs of both Penally and Gumfreston.

It seems not all Vicars had empty churches or dissatisfied congregations. I found him described as:

'. . . a tall, black, comely man, a good man, whose life was spent in the service of his Maker. Great fatigue and a fall from his horse threw him into a consumption of which he languished for some time. All churches tolled their bells on the day of his passing.'
February 13, 1686.

Amongst the other dwellings in the Hearth Tax, six are confirmed in the early surveys as: Bowen at **Trefloyne**, Thos Powell at **Whitewell**, Thos Rowe at **Court** House Thos Lewis at **Carswell**, Evan Williams at **Penholloway** and Mill, and Thos Waters at **Roberts Walls**.

Which leaves us to guess who occupied Tarr, Lydstep, Drusselton, Bubbleton, Palmerslake, and Holloway, all ancient houses that existed before 1600. The names we have for some of them in the first part of 17th century are not on the hearth tax list. The other names on the Hearth list, were likely rich Merchants, but we can only guess which houses they occupied.

Isolated cottages like Oxland, Out-of-Sight, The Pound, etc. with earth floors and stone, pyramid-built walls, and bread ovens, may not have qualified for inclusion, but were almost certainly in existence.

The earliest buildings are now ruins, such as St Deinol's Chapel and Rectory, the ruins of Whitewell, most of Trefloyne, Penally Court Leet, Lydstep Court Baron, Carswell, and Drussleton, They would have been amongst the superior houses, but other ancient buildings have survived, and have been continually inhabited to this day, such as Palmerslake, East Tarr, Frankleston, Middle Walls, Bubbleton, and Holloway.

Listing them historically, dates and descriptions follow.

14th Century – **St Deinol's Well and Chapel**
Both listed Grade 2 by CADW.

As viewed by Charles Norris about 1810.

The well is located beside the lane near the present Abbey Hotel.

The church advowson grant to the priory nuns of Aconbury in 1301 mentions a 'spring of St Theliai'. CADW says 'this is traditionally taken to be the present well ruin, and its proximity to the chapel ruins supports the identification.'

Others recognise the building as a Hall House:

'What is known as St Deiniol Chapel is a 16th century domestic building with vaulted undercroft adapted in the 19th century as a gazebo.'[7]

Fenton considered part of it to be a chantry chapel. There is a large 'flemish' chimney at the west pine end, unusual indeed if it was only a chapel.

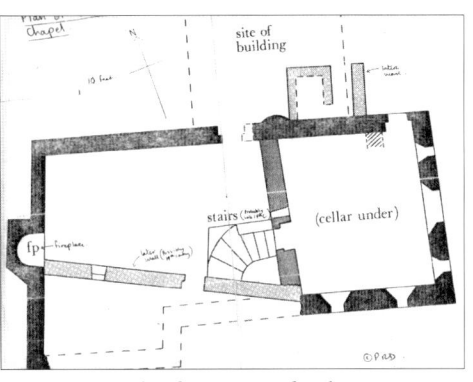

Plan from Warren family.

The eight nuns and their prioress may have thought that they would avoid the danger ahead by leasing their rectory in 1535, at a rent of £10.13s.4d, but at the Dissolution the lease was not honoured and, in 1541, the Crown leased it to Rice ap Morgan and Richard Merden of Cranbrook, Kent.[8]

These chapel ruins were much altered by the owner of the property, Miss Theodosia Robson, in the late 19th century, to create a fernery.

1326 – **Carswill (Carswell)** 'Cors' (Welsh) meaning marsh.
Listed Grade 2* by CADW.
Earlier of two ancient farm buildings North of the existing farm group and open to the public. Occupiers were:

1397 William Wyte.
1582 Watkyn Nicholl husbandry tenant, ref: Arch. Camb. 1898, p.71. Rev. G. Huntington, Rector of Tenby, canonised him in 1585. The lane in Tenby named after him is Wadin Nichol's Lane, it runs between Frog St. and High St. alongside T. P. Hughes shop.
1586 His widow Elizabeth Nichol. Tenby (dual) Charities until 1920.
1649 Leased to Thos Williams of Gumfreston.

---

7. W. Gwyn Thomas, RCAHM, for CADW description July 1964.
8. Richard Brinkley, 'Religion and Education 1660-1815', in *Pembrokeshire County History*, Vol. III, 104.

1659-60 William Lewis paid £6 to church wardens.
          Owen Williams of Tenby, butcher, paying rent of £14.
1707   John Marchant tenant 25 years. Rent £9.
1786   Frances Ankern.
1892   Cadwallader at Roberts walls.

Sold in 1920 by the vendors, Tenby Charities and the Church Charities of Tenby. It passed to the care of the State in 1982 and is now maintained by CADW. There is a very detailed description of Carswell in the paper Edward Laws wrote for Arch: Camb: 1867.

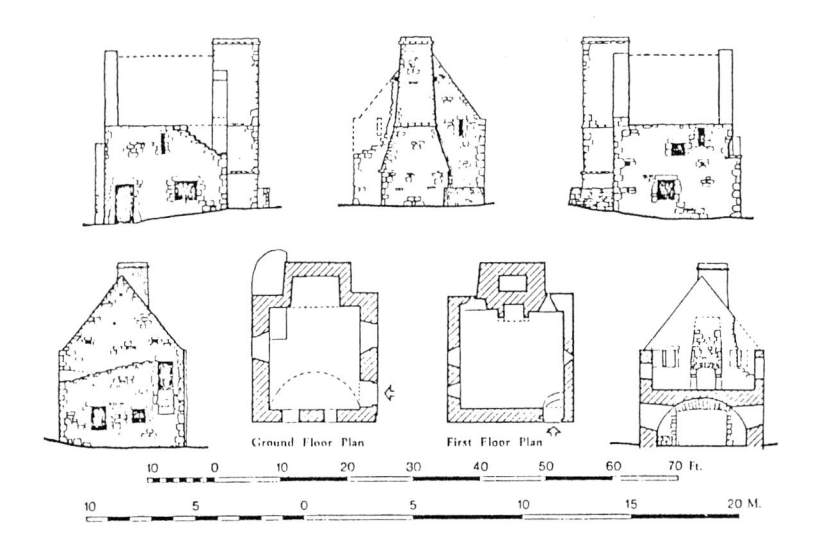

The plan of Carswell is curious, note there is a separate entry to each floor, but no internal access between. The first floor would have been reached by an external flight of stone steps.

The massive stone chimney is square, like the one at Palmers Lake, and would have served the kitchen or living area on the ground floor. The fireplace was huge and dominated the room. The upper floor was just one room lit by four slit windows in deep embrasures. A small but elegant fireplace with a stone hood carried on curving lintels and plain corbels heated the chamber. The roof was steeply pitched.

36

There is another building nearby which is equally ancient which consists of two stories but it is not open to the public.

Early C14th – **Trellwyn Treflyne (Trefloyne)**
A mediaeval great house.
   Home to 7 generations of Bowen family, descendants of Pentre Ifan.
   Thomas ab Owen held Trefloyne in 1491, descended to son Charles and then grandson Thomas who also held lands in Gumfreston, Templeton and Freystrop.
   Queen Elizabeth 1st leased the entire Manor to the Bowens in 1601.
   Thomas' son Charles was dead by 1640 and Charles' son Thomas, who played a somewhat ambidextrous role in the Civil War, had died by 1650.
   This ancient family seat was garrisoned for the King during the Parliamentary War by the Royalist, Lord Carberry, of the Vaughan family, High Sheriff of Carmarthen.
   The Bowens were strongly suspected of being Catholic, and all 150 men and 40 horses finally surrendered in 1644.
   Unfortunately, both father and son had made some costly errors in their affairs that culminated in the estate becoming the possession of the Philipps of Picton. Charles had charged his property with an annuity for life in favour of his second wife, Mary Tooley, in lieu of dower. He died before 1640 and she elected to take her dower, and being a Royalist, her interest in the estate was sequestered by the commonwealth.
   As well as this, amongst his debts, there was a sum of £2,000 due to Sir John Rouse of Worcester whose executor had extended to the estate.
   Charles Bowen's troubles did not end there, both his wife, her mother and sisters had been excommunicated for their beliefs.
   The Bowens were accused of often changing their persuasions when it suited them, but criticism was seen as treason.
   There was a petition to Parliament which explains the demise in importance of the ancient Bowen family, after the siege of Trefloyne.
   The footnote of the petition goes on to explain how Mr Bowen had had to flee his Mansion House for safety, and how his whole estate became prey to the enemy and was plundered to supply the garrison of Tenby. That Mr Bowen was now 'scanted of maintenance competent to his degree and unable to satisfy his creditors'. The plea was signed by:

Trefloyne ruins, circa 1835, from Tenby Museum.

Roger Lort of Stackpole   Philip Barlow   Sam Lort of Moor
Thomas Powell, son of Lewis Powell of Greenhill, Pembroke
Thomas Francis   William Phillips of Haythog   James Lewis
Po Mathias   John Lort of Prickaston   John Lloyd.

Dated Feb. 1646

His son, last of line Thomas Bowen married Anne, daughter of Sir Erasmus Philipps of Picton Castle and he died, in 1679, without issue. After the Philipps of Picton inherited the Manor, we see only tenants:

- 1714   Margaret Marchant (widow) who married William Phelps
- 1806   William Waters
- 1842   Robert Waters
- 1880   Pearce Llewellin Griffiths
- 1932   William Carey Evans
- 1938   John Henry Phillips.

The last owner occupants were Dr William Thomas and his family who took up residence sometime after the War.

Both he and his wife had been students at Aberystwyth University and from 1975 they allowed Trefloyne to be used for experimental field studies by the Department of Agriculture of the University College of Wales Aberystwyth. One of their sons, (Ian) D. F. Thomas, was on the threshold of a successful professional career when he was overtaken with blindness. Undaunted, he turned to farming, and achieved great success in growing early potato crops for VERBEYST the seed potato specialists in Bristol. He was often seen walking his greyhounds about the village.

The estate included the two farms Trefloyne and Penhoyle amounting to 314 acres of which 98 acres belonged to Penhoyle, which has become a conservation area with some fishing and forestry.

Trefloyne is now a Golf Club.

Circa 1362 – **Loudshope,** Lidsup, Lydstip, now **Lydstep.**

The large ruin that can still be seen, is often referred to as the 'palace' or 'place of arms'

There was a large upright long stone in the field adjoining which became the name of the Court Baron held fortnightly for Penally, it lies in the field called Longstone Park and is on the boundary of the parish.

It is tempting to think the Court was held at the 'palace' ruin but as R. F. Walker says, there is no evidence to prove this. It was however a rather grand dwelling and would have been very impressive in its time. There is reference to stone vault rooms at the 'palace'.

Nearby Lydstep Home Farm

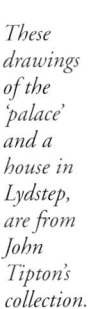

These drawings of the 'palace' and a house in Lydstep, are from John Tipton's collection.

must have been another messuage, perhaps not as ancient. It has not been identified or listed by any authority. The big kitchen and dining room off, were of ancient construction, and I remember the previous owner, Morran Boot, showing me how an early bed arrangement was built into the window space.

In 1601 Walter Rees Esq held 1 messuage and 70acres of land for 1/-.
1609: Walte Rice Kt.
1618: Will Barlow for 1/- and Whitewell
1689: Widow Taylor, late relict of John Taylor leased for 21 years for £12.10.0. John Taylor had leased for 3 lives paying heriot £1 and the same rent
1717: Barlow owned both Whitewell and Lydstep and William Powell occupied Meyrick owned West Lydstep and Nicholas Roach was his tenant.
1842: Ann Barlow owned 216 acres with James Parcell her tenant.
1882: Adam & Brooks lived in no's 1 & 2 Old Palace.
These were the last occupants.

It is more likely today, to think of Lydstep as the Mansion on the beach, but that fine house is comparatively modern. An earlier house had been built in that place by the Adams family.

John Adams of Lydstep drowned in his prime in 1798, a Fellow of the Linnaean Society and a promising conchologist.[9]

In 1888 Captain J. A. P. Adams, MP for the County, sold it to Sir Wynford Philipps: "wing upon wing was added and a long imposing drive made and hundreds of trees planted." There was a deer park in the grounds.

He restored many of the properties attached, with distinctive red pantiled rooves. These are particularly impressive on what used to be the stable block to the east of Lydstep Farm.

Circa 1324 – **La Torr. Tor. (Tarr)**
Listed Grade 1 & 2 by CADW.

The early name of La Torr meant 'high' for position and family.

There are now two properties known as East and West Tarr and also a Mediaeval House belonging to the group. The latter is listed as an excep-

---

[9]. Roland Thorne and Robert Howell, 'Pembrokeshire in Wartime, 1793-1815', *Pembrokeshire County History*, Vol. III, 383.

tionally well preserved small mediaeval tower-house of South Pembrokeshire type and the most complete surviving example, reminiscent of a £10 Irish tower. The ruin can be found at the rear of West Tarr farmhouse, which was first mentioned in a document of 1324 and is now in the care of CADW.

East Tarr (Great Tarr) has been permanently inhabited. It was freehold to David Nicholl in 1609 and to his son Philip after, who also held husbandry land at Roberts Wall. Followed in 1692 by David Williams, and then his widow.

In 1726 the distinguished family of Nicholas Dunn (of Crickmarren) held Great Tarr and was succeeded by his son John Dunn and children of his brother Thomas. The Dunn's held both East and West Tarr until sometime after 1786.

We have record of John Gwyther tenant in 1834.
Elizabeth Llewhelin in 1842.
Thos Bowen in 1881.
William Jenkins in 1923.

Finally, the Picton Estate sold it in 1908. It was sold again in 1986 as a substantial C19th country house (surely parts were C14th?), with 3 reception rooms, 6 bedrooms and 2 bathrooms plus 2 cottages and 6acres of land.

West Tarr is first mentioned in a lease of 1692 to Robert Smith for £28. Later held by Lewis Waters.

William Evans leased for 21 years in 1724.
and his son Henry in 1786.
John Gwyther leased in 1834.
Robert Gwyther in 1881.
Geo. Parcell in 1895.
Richard Edwards in 1923.

From 1932 Fred Williams held both, and his descendants still reside at East Tarr.

C14th– **Ruins of the Court House**
Listed Grade 2 by CADW.
'. . . the height of the surviving gable implies a building of considerable size.' Some of the walls were supposed to have been 7ft. thick.

Sadly, little survives to give any cohesive impression of the size or dignity of this ancient Court House estate. It had clearly been the core of the demesne.

A Court Leet was held there twice a year to deal with misdemeanors and disputes, at Easter and at Michaelmas. The Lord of the Manor, Thomas Bowen, held the Court House and Buildings and the land belonging to that house which amounted to about 80 acres valued at £4.1.2.

At the turn of the 17th century it became known as Penally **Court Farm** and valued at £10.6.0 to the next Lord of the Manor, John Philipps of Picton.

Court Farm before 1840 from the John Tipton collection.

1786 Land Tax reveals Thomas Rowe to be the occupier. He died in 1791 aged 64, and his son the Reverend Thomas Rowe succeeded. He had married Ann Elliot, sister to Lettice Elliot who had married the Rev. John Voyle. I only mention this fact to show how families were connected in the parish, and that it has always been so, in farming circles at least.

After his death in 1810 his wife leased the farm to William Waters of Knightson as well as Penhallway at a rent of £400 annually.

I imagine their son, George Waters, as a doctor in Haverfordwest, would have had no interest in farming. William Waters Esq, was a Mayor of

Tenby, and held both Court and Penhoyle from 1810. Mark Waters owned and lived at The Mount, Thomas Waters owned Hill, and Robert Waters farmed Trefloyne and Court Farm, in all, 600 acres.

This family were allocated 4 pews in the church.

The watercolour of Court and the marsh shows the roadway to the beach, clearly. The reeds and sedge in the foreground surround blue water and indicate that this was all a water meadow. Note the large gable end of Court Farmhouse before alteration.

In 1858 another house was built at Court Farm for a new tenant, John M. Griffiths a progressive farmer, show judge and member of the Welsh Land Commission. His story is told in chapter four.

In 1891 Sir Charles and Lady Philipps conveyed copyhold of Court Farm to J. W. Hawkesley Esq. for £121.18s. J. M. Griffiths was still the tenant.

The Picton Castle Estate auctioned Penally Court at the Royal Gatehouse Hotel in Tenby on September 26th, 1941; it was bought by Dr Charles Mathias. He leased it to Laurie Evans of Bubbleton soon after.

Circa 1362 – **Whitewill Remains (Whitewell)**
Listed Grade 1 by CADW.

An archaeologically important late mediaeval group of buildings, including one of exceptional size, comparable with the 'Palace' at Lydstep. The identity of its original owner is not known, but it appears to be an early manor house similar to Lydstep Palace. The principal building was a large structure with several apartments and an upper story. It had no vaulted or defensive arrangements. Again there were several cottages surrounding . . . CADW.

The hall had a fireplace at the south end and it stood over a vaulted undercroft. The wing, apparently of two stories, was also built over a vaulted cellar.[10]

In 1591 there was a 'deposition of Thomas Thomas of Whitewll touching a coalway from Hollyes Water by Kethins hedge along Holloway'.

1601 John Thomas & David Meredith holding 1 messuage 5 oxlands for 5d. Powell gent, holding ½ of 2 messuages for 10d.

---

10. Francis Jones, *Historic Houses of Pembrokeshire*, p.225.

1618 Wm Barlow took over from the late T. Powell for 5d.
1752 Lidstip and Whitewell sold to John Wogan, Philipps, Hook. Hamilton, Martin, Jones, Leather, Leach and Merchant & other purchaser.
1768 Mortgage of messuage of Whitewell to Wm Holcombe of Linion.
1788 Surrender for 800 years to John Phillips of Williamston.
1842 Laurence Cooke owned E.Whitwell and Wm Rowe occupied. There was Whitewell and Whitewill Green, they are shown as two holdings on the tithe account.
1881 Census shows Wm Smith at Whitewill and Thos Rees, the Green.

Unfortunately, the only drawing of this once great house is too faint to reproduce well.

Circa 1362 – **Palmereslake** and **Palmaryshlake** (in 1563) **Palmers Lake**. Today. Listed Grade 2 by CADW.

There were a large number of houses in this county that were originally built as Hall houses with a lateral chimney that dates them before the Reformation, though most of their character was lost when an overall floor was inserted in the late 15/16th century. He goes on to quote Palmers Lake as an example Mediaeval Hall House that has been permanently inhabited:[11]

> 'It is distinctive for its massive square chimney which is unique to this county, and has a formidable oven behind the fireplace. To this day it has original elm doors with old strap hinges on lugs. The roof is hewn purlin and trusses'.

It seems the better known, round chimney, is not remarkable and can be paralleled with many others in Devon and Somerset. It is the square chimney which is of unique interest and is not found elsewhere. This one, is of an extraordinary size when considered in relationship to the scale of the building it served.

---

11. P. Smith, *Houses of the Welsh Countryside*, 1988, p.286.

'It is clear we have a unique cultural pattern which may owe its peculiar style to the remoteness of Pembrokeshire from centres of Architectural fashion.' (P. Smith).

1692 Stephen Rowe tenant (owned by Lord Milford).
1726 Thomas Nicholas.
1786 Abrim Morgans.
1853 William Rogers leased it for lives though he lived on Hodgeston Hill, and his widow Margaret, aged 81, was there in ????. Her grandson was Wm G. Bowen, aged 16, who farmed it from 1895.
1908 Sold as freehold and 54acres.
1913 Joseph L. John
1947 T. Gill
1960 A. Seymour
1987 H. Wyn Jones, FRCDS.

C14th – **Old Quay** cottage Old Cai, Key, or Old Cay.
Described in a talk by Edward Laws in 1886 as 'a ruined house, used within the last twenty years, but from peculiarities of construction, appears to be an ancient structure.'

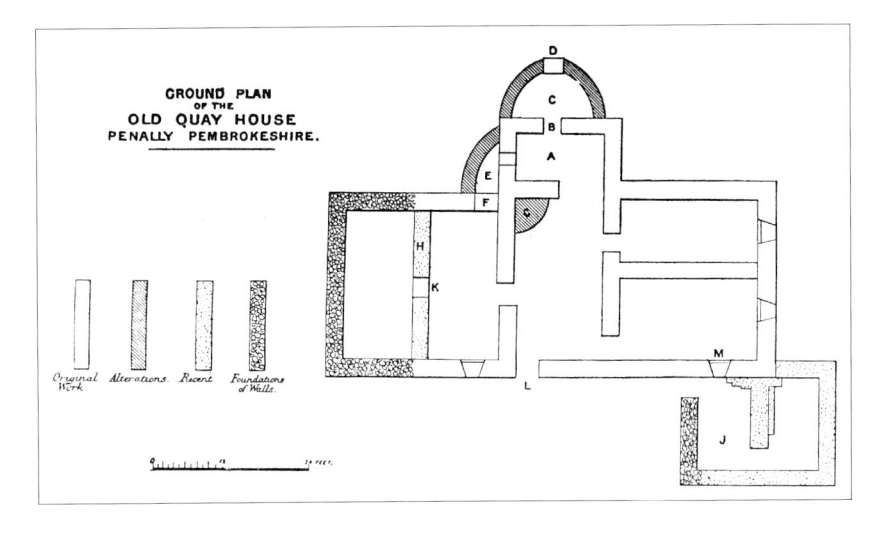

The house never had an upper story and its chief feature must always have been the large square chimney which towers over the cottage.

In this chimney was the only fireplace and when the house was young, the doorway must have always been open, for it was the only means of lighting the house.

Later a quaint little inglenook was added through a handsome pointed arch, and a window. Then another chamber and an oven. All the walls are thick and well put together with that excellent mortar known in the district as 'old castle mortar'.

'Old Quay is now, about one and a half miles from the sea, and a dugout 20ft. by 3ft. was excavated there and found to be similar to others in Pembrokeshire. I am disposed to think this cottage is of very considerable antiquity, dating back to a period when vessels discharged their cargo at the old quay before it was cut off from the sea.'

Only a part of this ancient cottage could have been a ruin, because in the 1841 census, Mary Andrew lived at The Cay. David Davies in 1851, and a much loved character in Catherine (Kitty) Gough in 1881.

May Beynon of Holloway described it as a thatched cottage with two rooms and full of charm, see page 67. Thomas Cray was resident in 1913.

It is known to have been occupied right up until the mid 1950's when tragically the body of its last resident, Heurtley Archibald Marmaduke Roberts was found in the house, days after he died. His story is told elsewhere in this account.

There were several dwellings at this place, shown on early maps.

C14th **Drussleton**, reference 1890 Tenby Guide.
The termination of the word Drussel-ton, as frequently in this country, gives us the name of the original proprietor, which in this case has somewhat of a Flemish sound.

Fenton suggests it was Norse surname, meaning a thrush, (Druss) and a close, (tun).

The Royal Commission in their Inventory of the County in 1925 said:

'Dru Selton was a single story house or cottage of which the fireplace and typical round chimney are the only remaining features of assured antiquity. It may well date back to the early 16th century.

Drusselton, Pembroke.

Now occupied by a poor labourer, formerly the dwelling of a substantial yeoman, or gentleman of moderate means.'

This was for many years home to the Beddoe family, shipwrights.

There were Beddoes at the Post Office in the village in the later years of 1853. In the 1841 Census we find William Smith who also farmed Bubbleton. In 1851 Sarah Johns and in 1881 George Williams.

Little remains to be seen of this dwelling today and it is a part of Bubbleton Farm.

The railway bridge over the roadway was named after it.

In the Court Rolls of 1610 onward, three Ash, and three Sycamore had to be planted every year, which gave the foundation for the site of today's rookery.

Circa 1627 – **Bubbleton**
Like Drussleton, this is also partly the name of the settler. The chimney stack is the sole relic of the original house, incorporated in today's modern farmhouse structure.[12]

12. Arch. Camb. 1887, p.146, E. Laws.

Customary Courts were held here at the end of the 17th century.

Early maps show several dwellings named Upper and Lower Bubbleton and Bubbleton Green which was free standing on a triangle at the roadside.

Occupiers were :
- 1692 Peter Nicholas tenant.
- 1726 Richard Evans.
- 1786 James Smith (owned by George Bowling) followed by Thomas Smith, followed
- 1853 by Benjamin Smith and William Smith.
- 1881 Seth Williams was at Lower Bubbleton. John Rogers at Upper Bubbleton and William Day at Bubbleton Green.
- 1895 Pearce Llewellin Griffiths owner.
- 1905 Joseph Protheroe tenant followed by Albert Protheroe in 1923.
- 1940 Laurie Evans followed to this day by his son Vernon Evans.
- 1948 Jo Morley Joseph at Giltar grove, formerly Bubbleton Green, previously farmed by Louis Thomas the farmer/author.

C16th – **Holloway** Farm.

A good example of a vernacular farmhouse. Permanently inhabited.

Illustration of Holloway from Tenby Museum (unknown artist).

Occupants:
1601   Morgan Voyle (and Frankleston).
1732   Arthur Williams (owned by Sir Hugh Owen of Orielton).
1786   Thomas Waters owner and occupier.
1842   Arthur Williams owned by Surgeon Major Charles Mathias.
1851   William Smyth (and Bubbleton).
1881   Henry Rees tenant.
1913   Thomas Beynon and Barclay Beynon.
1923   David Hinds and in 1932 John Hinds.
1959   Elwyn Harris.

When the new road by-pass was planned, it was to cut through the farm making things very difficult. The Mathias family offered an alternative farm to Elwyn Harris and sold the farmhouse, which was converted to The Paddock Inn, and the land adjoining was sold to a local builder who constructed The Paddock housing estate.

C16th – **Frankleston** and **Middle Walls**.
Not listed, but referred to in the surveys of 1601 and 1609 when Morgan Voyle was the freehold tenant of both, and in 1618 when Charles Bowen farmed them at a rent of 3s 4d referred to separately afterwards.

This early drawing of Frankleston is from John Tipton's collection.

John Hughes was the tenant at Middlewalls at a rent of £2.10s in 1692, and Mary Gwyther in 1786, and at the same time, John Fender was at Frankleston. There were a number of dwellings around and about, like Ducks Puddle (Common Hay) an early stone cottage of two rooms, sold in 1926. The first occupant of that, was the rabbit-catcher Charlie Evans.

It was thought to be the watering hole for drover's cattle in past times, and there was also a water pump at the roadside.

Understandable if you know the gradient of this hill.

There appeared to be two houses where Bank House is today, both September Cottage and Red House appear on the tithe map of 1842.

C16th Roberts **Walls**, is not mentioned by name in the surveys but we know it existed from reference in early transactions and other documents. The actual house may not have been built until after the farm was enclosed.

A great aunt of Mrs Shiela Morse drawing water at the well.

In 1570 Watkyn Nicholl took husbandry lands of his late father Philip at Roberts Walls.

The Census of 1841 puts George Williams there followed by Lewis Beynon in 1851.

Thomas Cadwallader in 1881 followed by his son Marchent.

When the Picton Estate sold off most of the farms in the parish in 1908 this one was purchased by Owen Jenkins of the Grove in Jameston, and inherited by his daughter Martha, who was my mother-in-law.

1718 is the first mention of **Crackwell** in Picton estate papers. Previously the references were Pepper park and Cooks' lands.

The house is pyramid built with walls of great depth at the base. It has been altered many times over the centuries. Laurence Cook leased it as one holding to a relative, Thomas Millard, who later bought it.

There is a large rookery below Crackwell, and the origin of the farm name is believed to be from 'Craeke' meaning crow, and 'weille' for spring. Fenton suggests the Norse Kraka for crow.

*   *   *

The farmhouses that were built after enclosure were traditionally 'two up two down' with a central entrance door and staircase opposite it, although variations would be an added kitchen, dairy, and porch. The house was usually placed at the centre of the farm with barns, etc. around and a driveway to the nearest road.

Blackrock Watch Tower is a building that has been described as a small fortress, fortified manor house or castle site abandoned in the 14th century. (CADW).

Today, it stands in a mature garden above Blackrock Quarry, but formerly this was an open headland overlooking Caldey Sound. Its purpose was more likely that of a beacon, and there is a tradition (without foundation) that it was used later as a snuff mill.

Caldey Island has always been extra-parochial, at least since 12th century, so that births, marriages, and deaths were recorded on the mainland, and many of these in Penally church. However, the Island, and that of St Margaret's, so near to Giltar Head would have been familiar and important to Penally.

St Margaret's was in fact included in the manor of Manorbier and Penally with 2 acres of pasture being worth 6s 8d rising to 13s 4d by 1618. A Penally girl called Mary Rowe married David Lewellyn in 1776 at St Nicholas. He owned and farmed Caldey, Thomas Kynaston mortgaged the Island from him in 1798 for £900. Llewellyn kept the dwelling house and half the rabbit profit, but over half a century later, his son George was still trying to claim £398 that had not been paid on the deal.

Cabot Kynaston held land and cottages in Penally village, and some of his daughters were christened in St Nicholas, one daughter and his wife, Louisa, as well as her two sisters are buried there.

Workers from Penally went over to Caldey for all sorts of reasons, especially during the boom of the quarrying industry. John Beddoes of Penally was one such; he had contracted to live on St Margaret's in a deal with John Davies, the owner at that time, but left 6 weeks before time. It must have been a very difficult and desperate way of life. St Margaret's actually had three families living on it in 1841.

Caldey has recently given up its ex-parochial status and become a part of the Tenby Borough. By doing so, it gains the advantage of joining the European Community, and the much needed financial aid which will help it survive as a unique sanctuary.

Over the centuries cattle were swum across the sound to the near beach of Whitesands (now the South Beach) and once landed, they would be marketed from Penally. This dangerous practice continued until quite recently.

Originally a priory, could this large building have housed several families?

St Margaret's Island by Chas. Norris showing one sizeable house.

Chapter 2

A Farmers Duel

Here, I want to interrupt the story of the development of the village, to give this account in its right context, and as an insight to attitudes at the time.

It was 1714 when Tenby Bailiffs instructed that a bridge be built across the Ritec to link Tenby to Penally and Manorbier. Eight years after the bridge was built, it was the scene of a truly dreadful murder. The story concerned two related families, the Athoes and the Marchants on the night of November 23, 1721.

Both families were yeoman farmers cum cattle dealers and could be regarded as more affluent than most. George Marchant, the murdered man, held Wall Park, and Western Close in Manorbier and his brother Thomas, who is thought to have held East and West Moor.

Penally Bridge after a storm a 100 years later by Charles Norris.

Their uncle, the perpetrator, Mayor Thomas Athoe and his son Thomas, who was their cousin, held land in Hodgeston. There is reference in the court rolls of litigation over many years involving Thomas Athoe senior. Altogether he seems to have been a bad tempered quarrelsome man. His sister had married John Marchant yeoman, the father of George and Thomas. This John Marchant was possibly a cousin of the John Marchant who farmed Carswell in Penally and whose widow leased Trefloyne in 1714.

The following account is taken directly from the *Cambrian Journal* 1863 (from the M.S in the collection of Joseph Joseph Esq F.S.A Brecon):

A Full, True and particular ACCOUNT of the Behaviour, Confession and last Words of THOMAS ATHOE, late Mayor of Tenby in Pembrokeshire, and Thomas Athoe his Son, who were Executed on Fryday July 5, 1723, at St Thomas's Watering in the County of Surrey, for a barberous Murther by them committed, upon the Body of George Marchant their Kinsman, in Pembrokeshire, Anno 1722

Published by Thomas Dyche, Chaplain to The King's Bench Prison. Price 2d.

As Murther is the most heinous of all crimes, so this, in the Ears of our Countrymen have been alarm'd almost since the Memory of Man, whether we consider the Inhumanity of the Fact from the nearness of the Relations who committed it, or from the Barbarity wherwith the Fact was committed. And, as the particulars relating to all unfortunate Persons, more especially Those who suffer Death, are the immediate enquiry of the Publick, I shall in the first Place, give some account of the Circumstances and Families of these unhappy Sufferers.

His Family consisteth of a Wife and Five Children; whereof the Second was Thomas Athoe, born in the Parish of Mannerbeer, and at his untimely Death, wanted but one Day to reach the 24th Year of his Age.

He always lived with his Father, and had been brought up chiefly in the Business of Husbandry and Grazing; and in the Time of his Father's Mayoralty, he serv'd as Bailiff of Tenby, aforesaid.

George Marchant, the murder'd Person and Thomas Marchant his Brother, were the Sons of John Marchant, Husbandman of the Parish of Mannerbeer before mention'd, and nephews to Thomas Athoe, Sen, being the Sons of his Sister, who married into the Family of the Marchants.

At this point there follows a long account of the prison Chaplain's dealings with the prisoners awaiting their fate, which I have omitted. He persuaded them both to make repentance, which they did eventually.
Young Athoe had fled to Ireland after the murder, but was brought back to face trial.
March 19th 1722: Thomas Athoe and his son were arraigned at Hereford Assizes, and because a verdict being brought in was Special they were brought to London and put in the Kings Bench prison in Southwark, and finally brought to the Court of the Kings Bench in Westminster Hall on June 22nd 1723 and there received Sentence of Condemnation.

The Case of the Two Athoe's
Upon the breaking up of the Fair, between the Hours of Ten and Eleven o'Clock at Night, the Athoe's very narrowly enquir'd of an Hostler at Tenby, which way the two Marchants went. In their Road Home, the two Marchants stopp'd at a Place call'd Holloway's Water, where they were overtaken by the Athoe's at the Bridge, as their horses were drinking. The night being very dark, the Marchants could not distinguish the Athoe's by their Persons, but upon his speaking, knew Old Athoe by his Voice.

The Marchants, to avoid the Mischief with which they were threaten'd by the Athoes at the Fair, and to do all that in them lay to prevent a Quarrel, they concealed themselves as well as they could, behind the Bridge, but the splashing of their Horses discovered them. As soon as the Athoe's came up, they began the Attack, especially Old Athoe, who would not be parted.

Drawing by author.

Principal witness was the dead man's brother . . .Thomas Marchant: 'they had used him in so barberous a manner that at the time of the trial, though it was four months afterwards, he was in so weak a condition that he could not stand and the Court permitted him to give evidence sitting.'

. . . The prisoners came thither to sell some cattle. A quarrel arising, young Thomas Athoe and the deceased George Marchant fell to fighting but the deceased had the advantage and beat young Athoe. Advised to bring action against George he said: "No, No, we will not take the law, but will pay them in their own coin."

In describing the attack, Thomas said: "*They both carried Ash sticks and old Athoe shouting Kill the dogs! Kill the dogs! Fell upon him (Thomas Marchant) beating him in a terrible manner and taking hold of his privitees pulled and squeezed him to such a violent degree that had he continued so doing a few minutes longer, it had been impossible for the poor man to have survived it.*"

Young Athoe, when he tired of beating the brother George, seized him by the privy members and tore out one of his testicles and calling out to his father, said, "Now I have done George Marchants business."

This horrible action occasioned a vast effusion of blood, but young Athoe's revenge was not yet glutted, for catching hold of the deceased nose with his teeth, he bit it quite off and afterwards tied a handkerchief around his neck so tight that the flesh almost covered it.

The Surgeon depos'd that the effusion of Blood upon this Occasion was not to be describ'd besides which, the very bruises George Marchant had received from the Violence of the Blows given him were sufficient to have killed seven men.

Mr Thomas Marchant was likewise attacked after the same villainous manner in his ***** and though he somewhat recovered, it is feared he is spoilt in those Parts.

'The deceased had 22 blows on his back, 3 great bruises to his head and 2 on his breast, his nose was bit off, and there was such an effusion of blood that it flowed two foot in the furrier.

Mr George Marchant was in the most grievous Anguish and Pain imaginable after the Assault, and expir'd in a few Hours.'

The Defense. The Athoe's pretended that they had been injured by the Marchants:

1st   In detaining an Estate from Them.
2nd That they, the Marchants, had bought some Cattle out of their Hands, at Wiston Fair, October 28th 1721.
3rd   That the Marchants had oppos'd their Elections.
4th   That Mr George Machant, the Murthered Person, had married the Sweetheart of young Athoe.

At their place of Execution the father claimed he was innocent of the crime laid against him and that he had not lifted up his hand against the Deceased.

The Son declar'd That he had no premeditated Malice against George Marchant but that, being Assaulted, what he did was in his own defence, that the Deceased having no Hair upon his Head to get hold of, the Damage he received must be by his own Handkerchief, which was tied about his Neck in two Knots, and he shew'd the Spectators, by pointing to his own Neck, in what manner he throtled him.

Thus ends the account.

*   *   *

On July 5th of that year they were taken by cart to the gallows which had been erected in an open space at St Thomas' Watering, a ford by a milestone of the Old Kent Road, used as a place of execution since 1539.

The Athoes were the last to be hung at this spot.

They were cut down and conveyed in two hearses to the Faulconers Inn and buried at St George's Churchyard, in Southwark.

Eight years later the Under-Sheriff who had had the miserable task of journeying with the two accused, well over a 100miles across wild countryside to Hereford, still had not been paid for his effort.

1730 April 16th. Petition of James Philips to be repaid his charges as under-Sheriff of Pembrokeshire in conveying to the Sheriff of Herefordshire by Habeus Corpus Thomas Athoe Senior and Thomas Athoe junior.[1]

Read and referred to Auditor Godolphin

---

1. Francis Green, Vol. 13, p.272.

Note the acceptance of such barbarity by society in those days in the following addition:

> As to the feelings of the Pembrokeshire farmers, we may take it for granted their sympathies were not with the Marchants, whose shabby trick would be brought up against them. It was a fair fight, two against two. Odds in favour of the Marchants. They were stronger men than the Athoes, both sides were mounted and armed alike with ash sticks.
> Of course, Tom Athoe made George Marchant fight.
> What else could a man of spirit do when he had been robbed of his girl and beaten in public.
> It was a duel, a farmers duel.

* * *

There were two prominent Marchant families in the area, one at Lamphey and the other at Carew. Studying their WILLS did not solve which was the family of John Marchant since each had children named George and Thomas. The Athoes also, are found in Manorbier and Tenby. Thomas Athoe Mayor of Tenby had five children, he was born at Carew but lived in Manorbier for 24 years.

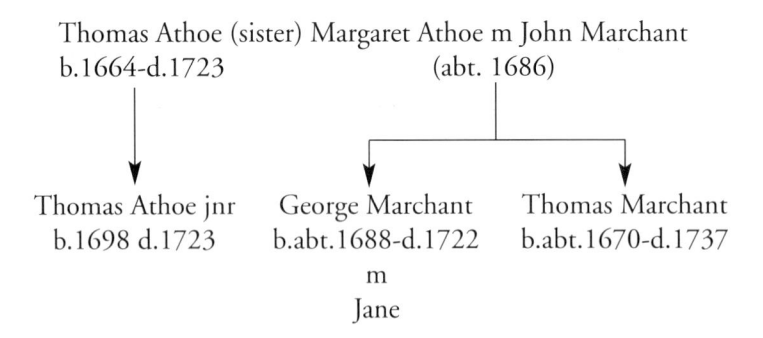

Thomas Athoe (sister) Margaret Athoe m John Marchant
b.1664-d.1723   (abt. 1686)

Thomas Athoe jnr   George Marchant   Thomas Marchant
b.1698 d.1723   b.abt.1688-d.1722 b.abt.1670-d.1737
                         m
                        Jane

I have not been able to find the burials of George or Thomas Marchant, it may be because they were thought to have been Quakers, in which case they would have been interred in the ground on which the Quaker rooms stood in Jameston, opposite the Swanlake Inn.

'Within the memory of old Tenby folk still alive, it was reported that on dark winter nights George Marchants' horse could be heard pawing the water by twin cottage bridge.'[2]

Finally, it is interesting to note that Joseph Joseph Esq. FSA. JP. and Fellow of the Society of Antiquarians, Mayor of Brecon 1861, from whose Manuscript the account was taken, is thought to be the Great, Great Uncle of the present Joseph family at Giltar Grove, which was Bubbleton Green in 1722.

2. *Cambrian Journal*, 1863.

Chapter 3

Georgian Penally

IT IS THE TIME OF THE House of Hanover, when a succession of Kings called George set the pattern for elegance and order. This is the time when the wealthy completed their education by doing 'The Grand Tour' of Europe, and returned with new ideas and technology. Land enclosure was now complete, and the 2,832 acres that made up Penally parish became 28 enclosed farms, on which farmhouses were built where they needed to be, and we have our first list of parishioners. We have examined the houses that already existed up to this time, but during this Georgian period, we will see the village forming about the church.

Land Tax records:

Holding	Owner	1786 Occupier	1791 Occupier
Rectory	Vicarial Glebe	Reverend	Rev. Thomas
Trefloyne	Lord Milford	Geo Williams	George Scale
Court	"	Thos Rowe	
Penholloway + Mill	"	Thos Rowe	Widow Lock
Tarr	"	John Dunn	Miss Dunn
West Tarr	"	Henry Evans	John Gwyther
Carswell	"	Frances Ankern	
Roberts Walls	"	Robert Lock	
Palmers Lake	"	Abrim Morgans	
Bubbleton	"	James Smith	
West Bubbleton	Geo Bowling	Geo Bowling	
Drusselton	Lord Milford	Morg. Ferrier	Benjamin Lewis
Cethin Close	"	M. Ferrier	Geo. Llewhellin
Middle Walls	"	Mary Gwyther	

Holding	Owner	1786 Occupier	1791 Occupier
Holloway	Sir H. Owen	Arthur Williams	
Frankleston	"	John Fender	
Lydstep	Madam Barlow	William Powell	
Whitewell	H. Barlow/L. Cooke	Wm Powell	W. Rowe/ Miss Parcell
West Lydstep	Meyrick	Nicholas Roach	
Penally	Laurence Cooke	John Mends	
East Whitewell	"	William Rowe + (Pepper Park & Bubb Park)	Evan David/ Stephen Griffith
Holloway for Penally	Thos Waters "	Thos Waters	
Saises Land	Saise	"	
East Penally		Ricard Wills	Geo Llewelling
Crackwell	Thos Millard	Thos Millard	
Little Crackwell	John Hooper	"	
New House	William Grant	Geo. Llewhelling & Martin David	
Frankleston	James Williams		

On the Estate map (overleaf) of 1768 drawn for Sir Richard Philipps Bart; there are a small number of plots both sides of The Court and at the east of the church which have individual names or numbers on them. They appear to be early building plots.

One plot seems to be where Fern House now stands, it is labeled Mr Hughes. Another, west of the Court, is marked Thomas Millar(d) and next to, is a plot with ? Williams. Notice the Road from Manorbier to Tenby, marked along the cliff, which was no more than a sheepwalk, and another road to Tenby via the Whitesands Beach

Many of the dwellings in the village are without deeds, even today, but by comparing building methods and styles, it is evident some of the houses we see to the north of the church, and those on the greens beside, were amongst the first dwellings, and may well have existed before 1800.

Also, Corse cottages, numbers 1 to 4 to the west of Court Farm, and Court cottage to the east.

A Murder of Crows – The Story of Penally

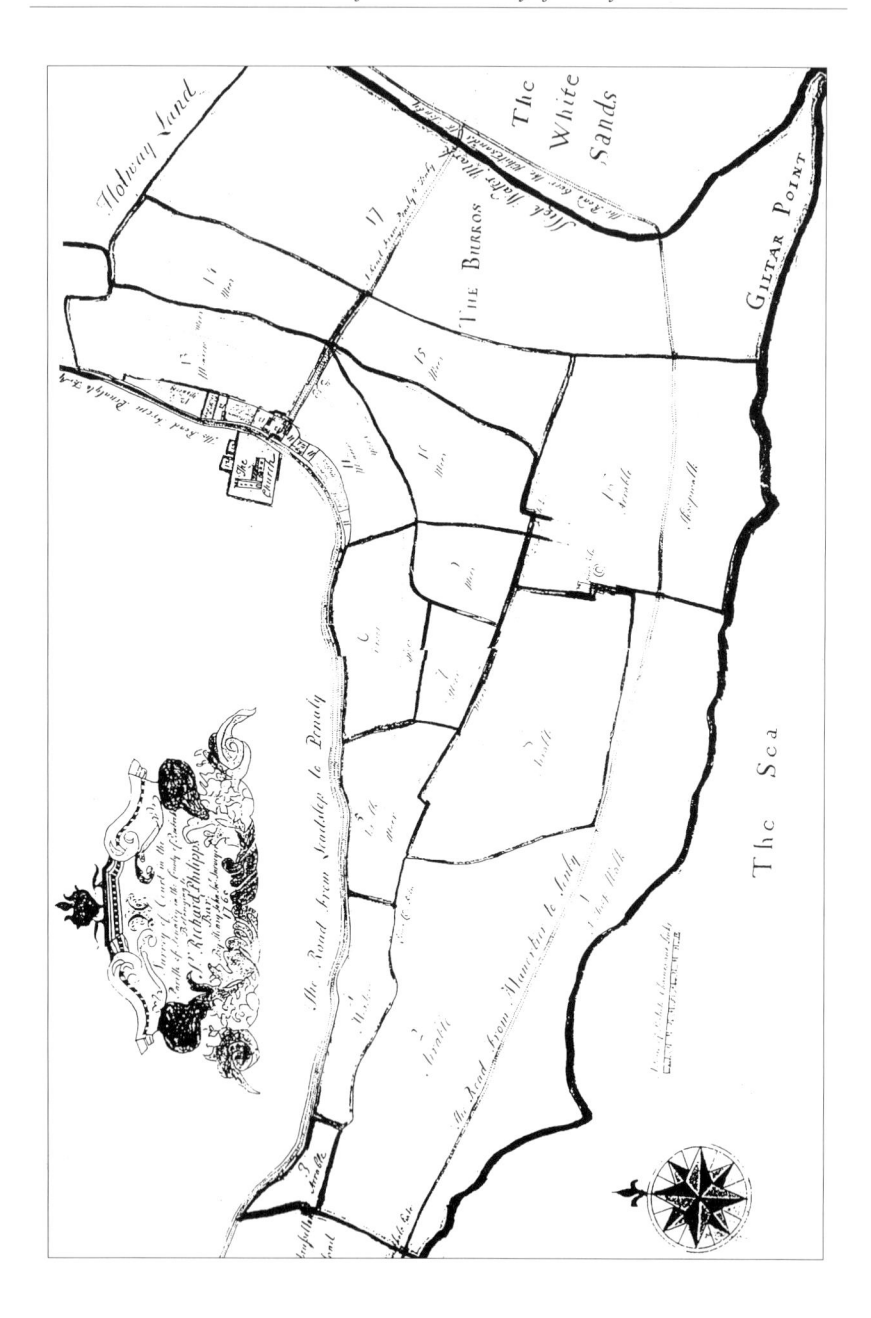

Village 1824

The tracing of the tithe map above shows Frankleston and Holloway farm complexes and two quarries to the east. The new Vicarage had a walkway linking it to the ruins and the old Vicarage, this was all Glebe Land.

The fields to the north where Penally House was to be built, all belonged to the Cooke Estate. Here were planted young trees, which were to become the woods behind today's Abbey Hotel. Was Cooke the builder of the Abbey? he owned the previous rectory.

The farmworker was no longer obliged to live in one of the out-buildings at his place of work. Cottages were probably built, as, and when, required, and heated with culm fires. These culm balls were made from the slime pits on the marsh near Holloway or from Drusselton, with anthracite coal dust added. People were now living close to the church where much of their social life took place, and by 1786 their children were near the new school Sir Richard Philipps had established in the churchyard.

The late 18th century, which saw those with money, delight in charitable and philanthropic works, is often referred to as the Age of Benevolence.

The Society for the Promotion of Christian Knowledge, known as SPCK, was set up, its aim being to establish schools throughout the country to spread Christianity, with a limited membership for children of the Church of England only. There was no room for nonconformists! The most outstanding SPCK member in Pembrokeshire, was Sir John Philipps who devoted all his energies, and most of his fortune to the cause. English was to be the language of instruction.

In the Parliamentary Returns it seems £3 was then paid yearly by the steward of Lord Milford, to a schoolmaster for teaching poor children of the parish. It stated, 'that in all probability this charity depended entirely on the pleasure of the then Lord Milford for its continuance.'

Many of the so-called teachers were themselves illiterate, some were physically dysfunctional, or very old indeed, and the classrooms often damp, or tiny. The teacher at Goodwick for example, was a one-legged sailor of seventy years of age, and at Uzmaston children were taught in a thatched mud hovel. Nevertheless, it was a start.

In Penally, a schoolmistress, seems to have been the first in charge, but 'being very old', she gave up teaching in 1824, having 'taught' upwards of 60 girls and boys.

They were taught spelling and reading we are told, but I do not imagine this compares with any teaching we know today. 'Some of them were taught writing and arithmetic, for which their parents paid the master extra'.

The next record of a teacher, is one William Owen, who may have taken over from the first lady. He was aged 50 in the 1841 Census, and lived at Frankleston. We know nothing more of the school until there was a Commisioners Enquiry in 1846, which is written up in the next chapter.

For the second or third son of a merchant or yeoman farmer however, there was the chance to improve their lot with an apprenticeship. An apprenticeship would entail a payment for a term of 5 to 8 years to a craftsman in a center like Bristol, for example. The same name families, repeated over many years, used this method of establishing their sons in some craft or profession

Interestingly, I found some early records dating from the 16th century and have listed some of the local name families:

1538   Martin Cavell of Penaleye was apprenticed to John Phillips of Bristol, a Bowyer, for seven years.

1558   John son of John Roawe Tenbighton (Tenby) to Robert Jones, a Tanner, and his wife Elizabeth for 8 years. Apprentice to have at the end 26 shillings and 8d.

1704   Jacobus Marchant son of Johannis Marchant of the parish of Carew, Grazier, posuit se apprentie Jacobo New, Shipwright, et Elizabethe uxor ejus pro septem annis.

1756   Stephen Rowe son of William of Loweston? Yeoman bound to Hugh ?vencombe, a gunsmith, and Elizabeth his wife for seven years.

1781   George Beddoe son of John Beddoe late of Haverfordwest, Skinner deceased, puts to William Heldor, a Hooper, and his wife Ann for seven years

1782   James Rowe son of Thomas Rowe of Milford, Mariner, put to James Martin Hillhouse, a Shipwright, and Mary his wife for seven years.

Thus sons could learn a skill or trade, and in fact 'apprenticeship' continued to be favoured even after a form of general education emerged. It was a costly business, but other than entering them in the clergy, how else could a farmer provide for numerous sons?

Typical working folk, 1750-1830.

Harvest time and other busy farm periods, saw many school absentees in those days, even until the 20th century. Note the reaper with a flask of ale in his hand. There was no tea for the ordinary man until the end of the 19th century, and coffee, even later. Everyone either brewed ale or simply drank water from the well.

The Wheelabout Arms stood at the Penally end of the Ridgeway, and because of its position, I would have thought it was a drover's pub, but there are no records to prove it. It was certainly the only alehouse in the parish in 1820. The house called Common Hay, which is nearby, once known as Ducks Puddle, was apparently also a watering hole for drovers.

John Owen of Orielton, the owner of Holloway and Frankleston, leased the Marshland in 1732. He started work on closing the salt marsh in 1811 and it eventually altered the topography of the neighbourhood more than any other single undertaking. On early maps it is evident how much land Sir John reclaimed from the marsh. An embankment wall ran from Black Rock to the cliff under Queens Parade, Tenby, and floodgates were installed to allow the Ritec to escape into the sea.

The limestone wall stood about 6ft high, part of its course can still be traced on the West Side of the railway embankment, which covers a few 100 yards of its length

The tidal estuary which had always separated Penally from neighbouring Tenby, still flooded a huge area twice a day, every day. P. H. Gosse, the Naturalist who spent much time in Tenby around the 1850's, said: "the sea rushes in at great speed, in the time it takes to count 55!"

With new enthusiasm Tenby Corporation paid £45 to Ambrose Smith, mason, to erect another bridge over Holloways water in 1817.

Wilson of Hen Castle said: "The bridge across the Marsh was building, the roadway was finished, and the parapet wall partly built. There was a breach in the sea embankment at which the tide came in, and, at the springs, came more or less over the bridge. I was riding home one evening when the tide was higher than usual, and I supposed I could go through the water on the bridge at the time, as I had frequently done before. But when about the center of the bridge it was so deep that my horse began to feel a buoyancy, got alarmed, sprang over the parapet on the sea side, and I had to swim him, and land near the Holloway Lime-kiln."

The phenomena of either the sea receding or the land rising has been observed in many other places and countries. "Several of the old sailors maintain that the rocks have grown nearer the surface. A smuggler, it is said, many years ago escaped from a Revenue cruiser over the ridge of rocks that at low water connects the islands of Caldy and St Margaret, where now a boat seldom ventures."

In 1822 Sir John sold the marsh, Holloway and Frankleston to Charles Mathias of Paradise House, Gloucester, for £9,845. The wall embankment that Sir John had built connected with a bridge over the Ritec. Part of it can still be seen, the railway line was built on top of it.[1]

The chart next illustrated (page 68), drawn in 1830, is clearly after Sir John enclosed the PILL and shows the steep gradient of the Ridgeway which is 300' above sea level in some places.

There is a drop of 150ft. on the south side of the Ridgeway to the road below, which was then often waterlogged and impassable.

The short dark lines in Caldey Sound indicate where the oyster beds lay, in fact they contained the biggest oysters in Britain but were already in decline through over fishing by this time.

---

1. Conveyance D/EE/L/1/16 HRO.

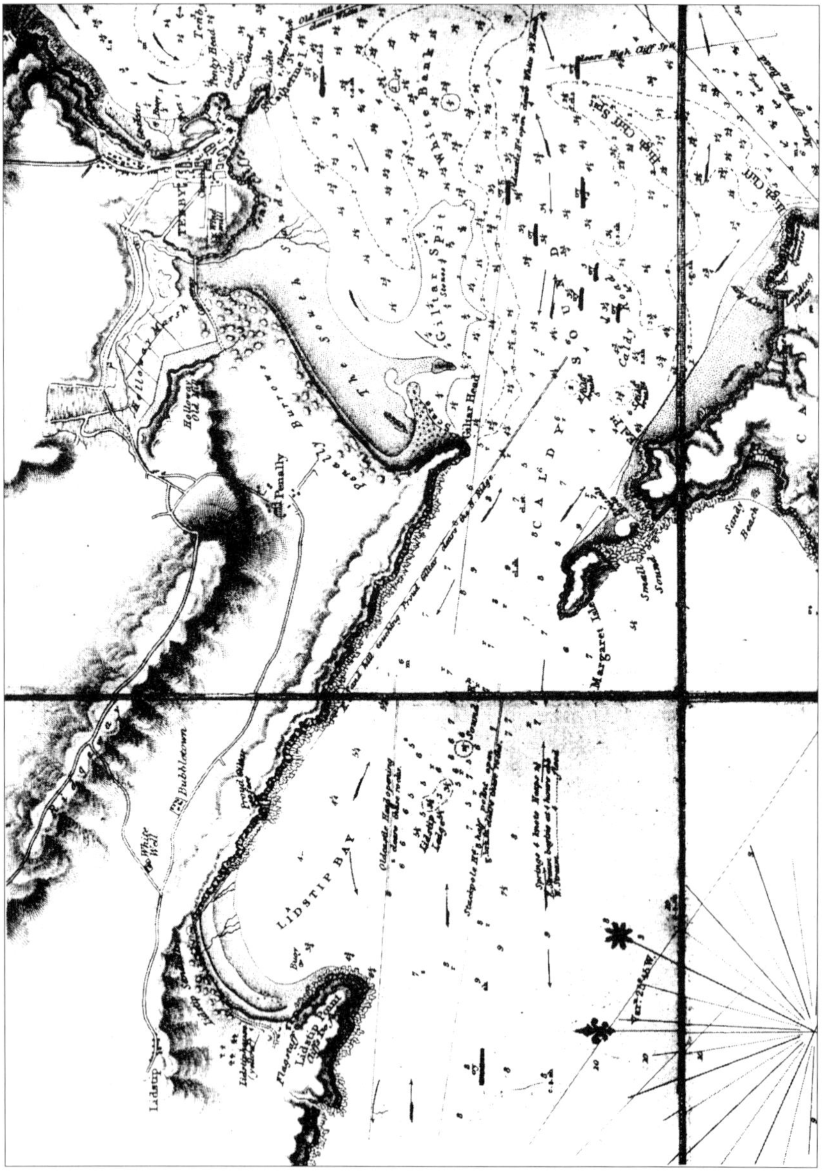
TENBY
Penally
LIDSTIP BAY
Giltar Head
Giltar Spit
White Bank
Holloway Marsh
Bubbleton
Lidstup
Margaret Isle
Small Sound
Sandy Beach

In 1836, a severe storm battered the wall and 200 yards of it breached on the Tenby side, it was repaired in 1840 but the tide continued to cause problems.[2] A timber merchant, who had his storage yard near the present entrance to Quarry cottages, floated a timber-laden ship through the gap in the yard. This incident stirred Mathias into action. He gave notice to the merchant to remove the ship and sent men to re-build the wall. The railway was eventually built on top of it.

> "There are those now living who can remember the time when vessels proceeded nearly a mile over what is now pasture land, as far as the place known as Holloway Quarry; that vessels came up and discharged their cargoes at a quay situated at the bottom of the Pill field, near where the at boats were frequently taken to St Florence, a distance at present of full four miles from the sea.
>
> Two posts are still standing upon the Marsh road about a mile and a half from Tenby, which were placed there to mark the depth of the water at Spring Tides. Vessels were laid up, high and dry for the winter during the last 100 years, beneath the hill near the station."[3]

From this it will be seen how much water played a part in holding up the development of Penally, in fact, until the by-pass was completed, the road and bridge at Kiln Park still flooded sufficiently at times to cause road traffic to divert around Ivy Towers and north to New Hedges to get to Tenby.

Overleaf is a watercolour by Fanny Price Gwynne, dated about 1850, which shows clearly how Penally appeared as a headland, surrounded as it was by water, and viewed from the burrows.

These burrows too, were less formidable than they are today. Note the original gable end of Court farm just below the church, and how few trees there were.

However, to return to the late 18th century, few of the houses you see in the 1850's water colour of Fanny Price Gwynne overleaf, had been built at that time, but it shows the ever present water around the village.

---

2. Note from Edward Laws article in *Tenby Observer*. He was the grandson of C. Mathias.
3. Fanny Price Gwynne, *Tales and Traditions of Tenby*.

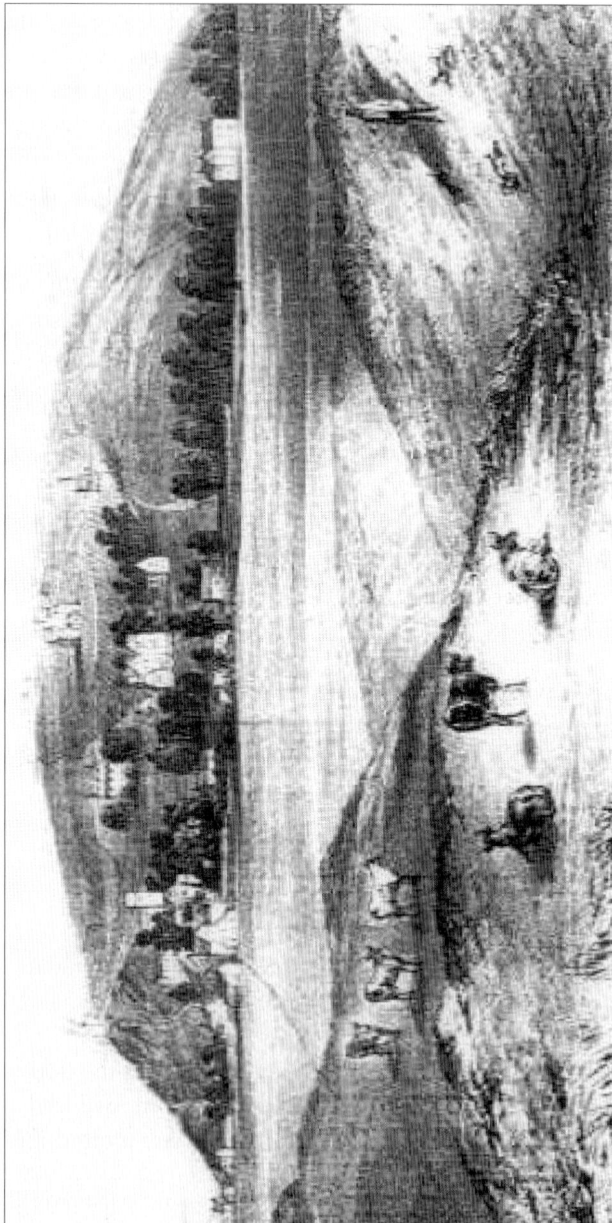

Early parish records have vanished, or were never kept, even though it was mandatory from 1538. Neither were there graves with headstones until late 18th century. So we have little information until 1738, when the existing parish records show which of the parishioners attended church, to register a birth, to be married or to record a death.

The first entry in the records is when John Williams was the incumbent and he wrote very briefly as will be seen. Many of the names found there seem familiar. Unfortunately, they were written so faintly it was pointless trying to photocopy them, but they start on the first page:

> John the son of William Grant baptized August 1738
> Alice the daughter of Alban Lavers[4] baptized 27th August 1738
> Laurence Cook was interr'd the 14th day of October 1738
> George the son of Thomas Rowe was interr'd the 5th day of November
> Richard son of Richard Rowe baptized November 1738
> John the son of William Grant interr'd October 1738
> Alice the daughter of Alban Lavers also interr'd 1738

Other entries I noted were:

> John Edwards was interr'd April 1748
> Robert Waters married Mary Rowe 20th August 1748
> Thomas Harry of Palmers Lake buried 1757
> Rees Purver aged 101 was buried December 26th 1759
> Elizabeth wife of Nicolas Dunn yeoman buried 1761
> Lewis Harry of Carswell farm buried 1764
> William Vaughan was killed with a cart and buried in 1796.

Local drownings are recorded, along with events on Caldey.

The Marriage Banns book starts with praise of the character of the Reverend John Williams, 1754 to 1774. It is interesting to note the uniting of the local farming families, and often the same witnesses appear over and over.

---

4. Alban Lavers was a Blacksmith from Jameston. Originally French, his name was La Viers.

Some of the surnames are repeated for a span of more than a 100 years, which suggests that people did not travel far to find a partner.

A great many of the farming families were related to branches in Manorbier and St Florence, and all to each other.

In 1793, the bailiffs instructed a kiln to be built on the western side of the Pill fields. This was not just one ordinary kiln, but the magnificent set of structures you can see today at Kiln Park which were to become very important indeed to the local economy.

In 1819, John Hughes, then a young man of 26 years, arrived as the newly ordained vicar from St David's. His younger brother Henry was vicar of 'Manorbeer and rector of Hodgeston' and lived with him at the old Rectory.

At this time, St Nicholas had an average congregation of 150 souls including 55 children. The whole parish consisted of 346 inhabitants. He was to serve the community for 54 years. What changes he saw!

When he arrived in Penally, the country had just seen the destruction of Napoleon's Grand Army and there had been the great Victory of Nelson at the Battle of Trafalgar in which our own Captain Hugh Cook had fought so valiantly.

The dissolute King George IV succeeded in 1820.

During the next fifty years we see small industry developing like the brickwork's in Trefloyne lane that Paxton, the great architect of Georgian Tenby, needed for his building programme. There was a gravel pit at Lydstep, clay and sand were dug at Middle Walls, there may also have been some boat building, over a 100 men were employed at the quarries. There was work too for builders and carpenters for workers families who needed houses to live nearby.

All of which meant employment for masons, stone cutters, hauliers and labourers. Socially, people were now, much more 'civilised.'

There was more affluence, language was more refined, people practiced good manners and cleanliness was next to godliness. St Nicholas, being the religious center of the new village, was also the social center, the meeting place for neighbourly exchanges, romantic assignations, gossip, business, and public information.

Vicars, too, were better educated, and were seen as father figures in the community. They were on a social level with the squires and landowners.

In Penally, the Vicar was better paid than ever before, his living amounting to £81.10.5d which included tithes, glebe land, and surplices. He was the pastoral carer, the village comforter, and sometimes even the village doctor, but most importantly, parish records were properly recorded.

A new Rectory was planned in 1822 and £225 was raised by mortgage to the Bounty Office on Dec. 4th. John Hughes' income by this time was £181.6.0 gross, plus a house and coach house.

The Reverend John and his wife Sarah, created a lovely garden in the new vicarage which was an acre in size, they no doubt enjoyed their beautiful house and all the comforts they could now easily afford, and a more lavish social life.

He had met Sarah Bilsborrow, whilst she was holidaying in Tenby, and they married soon after, she was eleven years older than he was, and they lived with his two younger brothers and four servants. Sadly, they had no children, and Sarah died in 1850.

Brother Henry continued to live with him, they were very fondly attached, but he too died in 1857. Two years later, John married the daughter of Samuel Fox Esq who was head of an old Derbyshire family.

The Reverend Hughes made it his business to be involved with the development of the fast growing hamlet of Penally and was Chairman of the Poor Law Guardians. There had been no Sunday school and only one Sunday service. He started a Sunday school in an old building on the higher side of the churchyard, which was succeeded by a day school.

He continued to preach in Penally church into his 80th year.

His colleague at Gumfreston, the Reverend Gilbert N. Smith, having arrived at much the same time, was a larger than life character, about the same age as the Reverend John Hughes. He had a wife and five children, and was quite eccentric in many ways. However, he is best remembered as a Pembrokeshire Antiquary who made seriously important 'finds' in both the caves at Hoyles Mouth and at Eels Point on Caldey, which have formed the foundation of the Museum in Tenby. He died in 1877.

I mention him, because the lifestyle of these two clergymen illustrates how times had changed, the fact that they were both scholarly men and could afford to indulge interests outside the church.

John Hughes' interests did not run to caring for the appearance of his church however, 'allowing the grass to grow, and his cattle to roam at will.'

The end of the Georgian period is sometimes called The Age of Reason, and certainly there was a greater emphasis on learning.

For the gentry at least, there was time for leisure pursuits like hunting, and shooting, collecting shells and writing poetry. The ordinary labourers still worked from dawn till dusk with no holiday, it would be a long time before they enjoyed a half day on a Saturday. They were, however, healthier and with a better life expectancy.

A famous Georgian called Charles Norris 1779-1858, happily for posterity, recorded views around and about Tenby, and although he did not live in the village, he chose to bury his wife Sarah, and many of their children, who seem to have died very young, at St Nicholas. He was a great topographical artist.

John Tipton, in his booklet on Norris, describes him 'as a gentleman artist who arrived in Tenby in 1805, and was able to capture its rebuilding at that time, as well as surrounding areas like Penally. His drawings give us an important record of that period.'

By all accounts, he was something of an eccentric, and very outspoken.

He built Waterwynch in 1817 to house his growing family of eleven children, seven of whom died in a short space of time. Sarah, his wife, died two years after the birth of the last child. Charles then married his housekeeper Elizabeth Harris in 1833 and they produced three more children.' He had lived there for forty years.

Recognized as an intelligent man, Norris was charged with inspecting the Tenby Churchwardens accounts with his close friend the Reverend William Tuder. They reported abuses, corruption, and misappropriation, and the Rector was not pleased, which may have been the reason Norris chose to worship at St Nicholas and bury his family there. Tenby Museum holds about 200 of his works, but the bulk of the collection, sadly, are in Cardiff Public Library.

Undoubtedly, the greatest influence on the formation of the village was that of the Cooke family who are recorded in Pembrokeshire as early as 1347.

In this parish they appear in 1601 with Phillip Cooke having husbandry lands, referred to as Cooks Lands and Cooks Hays.

David Cooke followed his father, Phillip, in 1618, and his widow Jenet who had been born in Penally, took his place as owner/occupier.

Laurence Cooke, their son, followed, he married Susannah, and died in 1738 and is buried in Penally.

Their son, Lawrence junior, is the point at which this family exceeded itself and founded a dynasty that would alter the appearance of the village entirely.

He married Margaret Shorting, a well-connected, wealthy young lady. Her mother Martha, was the daughter of Thos Hammond whose wife Martha, was sister to Henry Lloyd Esq, of Llanstephan Palace who was the last male representative of that ancient family.

Over the years, the Cookes consolidated their holdings in the parish, and virtually set about building the village. Lawrence was Mayor of Tenby in 1782 and again in 1790 and there is a plaque in St Mary's church in Tenby:

'To the memory of Lawrence Cook Esq, who died 1792. Magistrate'.

They had a family of six children, Hammond and Susannah died in infancy, and Sarah died in 1804. There remained, Captain Hugh Cook R.N. (illustrious hero) his one remaining sister, Martha (a spinster) and a brother Rev. Thomas Shorting Cook.

Hugh had entered the service in 1784, was made a Lieutenant in 1793 and was promoted to Commander in 1806. When Sir William Paxton died in 1824, the sons sold the Paxton property to Captain Cook. A Chancery suit followed with heavy law expenses on Tenby Corporation even though he was a member of the Common Council himself.

When he died in 1834, he left a charity to seamen and their widows in Tenby, and Trafalgar Rd and St Domingo were streets named after his great battles. He had served with Captain Bligh of 'the Bounty' fame when he was Rear Admiral, and his contacts through Naval Service, and connections with the East India Company, induced others to discover beautiful Pembrokeshire and settle here, once suitable houses were built to accommodate them.

His sister Martha, owned a good deal of land and property in her own right. She lived in a large block on the corner of Frog St. and St George St., where Piper's now stands, that stretched to the Five Arches in a square. She also owned the corner property opposite and many houses in St Julian St.

It was she who found her brother's last WILL and Inventory in a trunk of his, a year later, and in this, his heir was found to be one Charles Wells R.N. of Hampshire. I believe he is referred to as 'nephew' in an earlier draft WILL. Charles was then living in India and no doubt it took time before he received the news and could make arrangements to return home. In the meanwhile, Hugh's sister Martha was given powers of Administration.

Whilst he left reasonable bequests to his brother and sister, to granddaughters of his two Uncles, to the four daughters of Sir Robert Phillips, a charity to the poor of Penally and another to Tenby, these were insignificant amounts compared to the value of his estate.

The land and properties in Penally and elsewhere, plus the Bonds to the value of £9,000, and mortgages and money owed to him of another £2,000, would make him by today's standards, a millionaire.

Hugh Cooke had also been a friend of John Tuder of Tenby and he was given 'fields for his life'. Several 'Tuder' children were born in Penally, but I cannot be sure where the family lived.

More is written of Charles Cook Wells in the next chapter. Martha presented one of four pieces of silver plate to St Mary's Church in Tenby, measuring 11inches and 26oz weight.

Some of the buildings that existed in this Georgian period are:

The **Lime Kilns** 1793 – Listed Grade 2 by CADW. Origins obscure. A set of six large kilns in hammer-dressed limestone with rounded corners, and all, steeply vaulted.

The celebrated Architect John Nash has been traditionally associated with the building of these magnificent kilns, but there was also a colliery blacksmith of that name in 1808, living in Saundersfoot. By 1861 he was a person with substantial property. It is possible that the coming of the railway as a consequence of the Black Rock Quarries, is where credit to John Nash may be due.

The following explanation of this new resource from Arthur Young Touring in Wales shows how important it was to farming.
Lime[5] is the common manure. It is carried in panniers on horses even to Carmarthen:

---

5. Arthur Young, *Touring in Wales.*

4 barrells is from 4 to 5 Winchester bushels
5 barrells = a load
3 to 4 loads to the acre for 3 crops

Priced at the kiln at 3 shillings the load. It is burnt with culm raised within ¼ ml of the quarry. They burn from April to September never in the winter. The effect of it is very great on all soils.

Michaelmas Cottage
Sited in the church grounds to the north. Originally the Poorhouse.

The old school of 1804 was built on its foundation. The building was given to the parish by the guardians. There was a building at its rear which was included, and altered in 1855 to a new schoolroom by the Reverend Hughes. The rest of it became the schoolmaster's house. It was the property of the Church of Wales until 1965 when it was bought by Penally Parish, and given its present name.

1824 – The Old Vicarage
Listed Grade 2 by CADW as a good house in late Georgian style.

It retains much of its Georgian character. Built for the Rev. John Hughes under the provision of Gilbert's Act.

In F. P. Gwynne's book of 1852, it is described as: 'a modern house, and has a garden laid out with much taste.'

Originally, it stood in an acre of grounds running to the west with walkways to the Chapel ruins and original vicarage.

This is an early Charles Norris drawing, showing the house and its proximity to the church through the garden.

Admittedly, it is a poor reproduction, but one can just make out the stables on the right.

It remained the vicarage until yet another new Vicarage was built in the grounds of the old, then this Georgian house was sold in 1956. It was converted to a thirteen bedroom summer letting property by the family of William Grey.

C.1834 – **The Cottage** – also known as 'Old Palace Gardens'. Grade 2 CADW.

Large house of the early 19th century on foundations of an ancient cottage, the kitchen survives at the rear and the floor level is above that of the rest of the house.

The remarkable copy below, of another Norris watercolour, was labeled The Place with the added note, 'taken down in 1838'? (Norris drawings are traditionally recorded as 1810-13.)

Church Hill Cottage. From John Tipton's collection.

I believe it to be the original house which must have been rebuilt a few years earlier than 1838, since Hugh Cook died in 1834 and it was occupied for some years up to 1841 by a lady of Independent means. The architectural style is late Regency, which would date it at around 1830.

Although it is hard to decipher the writing of the ennumerator in the April 1841 Census, it appears that an Agnes Dinchey or Dineley was the occupant.

She moved to 4 Lexden Terrace in Tenby, a gentlewoman from Cornwall. As will be seen in the Schedule of Deeds (page 80), Hugh Cook them leased it to the Misses A. and F. Bond.

I remembered seeing a pew allocation to Bond of **Churchill** in 1851, and realised that the house must then have been called by that name. Miss Ann Bond died in 1864, and her sister Frances continued to live there. Interestingly, another sister was Louisa Kynaston, widow of Frederick Kynaston of Caldey. She also lived at Churchill after she was widowed and died in May 1878, Frances died the same year in December and the *Tenby Observer* advertised the SALE of the house in 1879.

The parish register mentions a child born to George and Catherine Brown of Churchill in 1854, he was an Assistant Surgeon in East India Co. Service. Again, note yet another member of the E. India Co. in the village, it seems all through the 19th century Penally had some connection to this company, they must have been a tight knit community.

In 1880 it was assigned to Mrs Elizabeth Voyle and was always known thereafter as 'The Cottage'. The garden once held many interesting plants brought back from India by members of the Voyle family.

Elizabeth Voyle's daughters Amy and Adela lived with her, and they were followed by her brothers two children, Urith and Dolores Voyle. None of them had issue, and when Miss Urith Voyle died in 1991 she gave 'The Cottage' to the National Trust.

From personal knowledge, until 1991, I can say that the property had not been modernised in any way and remained in the charming time warp of the 19th century. The green in front of the Cottage was sold to Clement J. Williams of Penally House.

Urith (front) and Dolores about 1970. On Penally sands.

Barclays Bank Trust Company Limited
South Wales Regional _____ OFFICE

SCHEDULE OF DEEDS, ETC.

PROPERTY __'The Cottage', Penally and land known as 'Old Palace Garden'__
Tenby, Dyfed
TRUST TITLE __Miss Urith Elliot Voyle Deceased   10/4491__

DATE	YEAR	DESCRIPTION OF DEED	PARTIES	
10.2.	1834	LEASE AND COUNTERPART	H Cook Esq	Misses A Frances and C Bond
14.7.	1841	CONVEYANCE	Miss C Bond	The Misses A & F Bond
30.3.	1880	ASSIGNMENT	Thomas K Neir Esq	Mrs E Voyle
	1885	ABSTRACT OF TITLE		
16.5.	1885	COPY AGREEMENT	G Warren Esq	Mrs E Voyle
12.6.	1885	CONVEYANCE	Messrs W.de G Warren & G Thomas	Mrs E Voyle
10.2.	1906	DEED OF GIFT	Mrs E Voyle	Major H E Voyle and Misses A C & A G Voyle
2.12.	1912	CONVEYANCE	Messrs G W Williams & O H Williams	Mrs S D Power
7.5.	1915	VALUE FOR PROBATE	re. Elizabeth Voyle Deceased	
1.7.	1915	PROBATE OF WILL OF	Mrs E Voyle Deceased	
27.3.	1918	COPY LETTER	from Chapel Bay Fort with others attached	
10.7.	1918	DECLARATION	by J H Owen Esq	
14.7.	1918	CONVEYANCE	Mrs S D Power	Miss A C Clyle & Lieut Col. H E Voyle
3.2.	1939	DEATH CERTIFICATE	H E Voyle	
9.10.	1948	RECEIPT FOR REDEMPTION OF TITLES		
3.2.	1951	PROBATE OF THE WILL OF	Amy C Voyle Dec'd	
12.7.	1952	ASSENT	by R.E.L. Mathias-Thomas	
4.1.	1975	DEATH CERTIFICATE	Miss Dolores Joan Voyle	
		1 PLAN		

Received the above deeds and documents this   day of   19

NOTE.—Every distinct set of Title Deeds must be accompanied by separate schedules (in duplicate).
Every document must be separately specified, the oldest document coming first.

C.1800 – **Penally Abbey** – Listed Grade 2* by CADW. CADW say 'The Abbey is North East of Penally Church. First mentioned in 1803. Listed as a well detailed Gothic house around 1800.'

Penally Abbey. (Photo: Gareth Davies Photography).

This is perhaps the most interesting building of size in Penally Village. There has always been some mystery surrounding its origin and CADW throws little light on the subject.

Examining the architectural styles, my impression was 'Gothic Revival' of the time of William IV. After the Napoleonic war there was a break up of tradition and a revival of the romantic school.

It was a period referred to as the 'battle of the styles'. The abundance of ogee curves, and other pseudo mediaeval details, plus the armorial crest placed in the wall, are characteristic features of this period.

As to the origin, Richard Fenton writes in his *Historical Tour through Pembrokeshire*, page 243:

". . . in a field about two hundred yards to the north of the church are the remains of a building, which from its form and position, I should take to have been a chantry chapel. *The house that the clergyman now lives* in bears marks of it *having been* a very dignified mansion, and of great extent, by portions of ruined walls in various directions and covering much ground."

Fenton's tour took place at the beginning of the 19th century and I am content to believe that when the nuns abandoned their gift, during the

Dissolution of 1534 it all became the property of the Church of England and the dignified mansion that Fenton referred to, returned to its original use as the clergymans house.

In the Hearth Tax of 1670 the Rev. Ethelred Wogan had two chimneys, one still stands in front of the hotel. There is another at the chapel ruin and the two properties would have belonged to the Welsh Church Commission, a single owner.

The earliest Tithe Maps show two distinct properties in the area of the present Abbey building, and the later O.S. Map of 1907 marks a path linking the present Old Vicarage through the grounds around the ruins and to the 'Abbey'. The 1841 tithe accounts for 11acres of Glebe land (including the church and graveyard) and lists the owner as Charles Cook Wells.

The present building must have been constructed after the new vicarage was built in 1822/4, and the style would place it between 1830-50. It is feasible that parts of the foundation were original walls from the earlier rectory.

John and Anne Tuder, the important Tenby family, lived in 'a Penally House' according to Parish Records, when three children were born to them between the years 1831 and 1836. He was a Lt in HM Navy. John Tuder had been given 'fields' for life by Hugh Cook, but the tithe map is so indistinct that field and plot numbers are ambiguous. Did that family live in it?

The first occupant I can trace was a Mrs Mary Robson, of Doncaster, a widow with two daughters, Theodosia and Jane, who lived there after 1841. She died in 1851, and her daughter Jane two years later. They are buried at St Nicholas. She held pew number 11 for 'both houses' she also rented Westley Park which was where she built The Glen on old foundations. There was a law suit taken against the builder she employed for under-quoting the cost of building The Glen. This must have been 'the other house' referred to in the pew allocation.

Looking at the early drawings of the 1840's and 50's, it is apparent that the house now called the 'Abbey' differs in style from the house we see today.

At that time it had two gables facing East, whereas today it is altogether more complex, and the 1860's could be the time when further alterations were made and the name was added along with the armorial crest.

The crest high on the wall is interesting. Thomas Lloyd who wrote *Lost Houses in Wales* has attributed the heraldic device to that of the Bosanquet family, but quite how it fits into the question of who built the house is not clear at this point. There was a prominent family called Smith-Bosanquet in Norfolk and we find the Rev. John Smith of Norfolk in residence in 1873 along with his son and five beautiful daughters. It is about this time the house was called 'Abbey' and may well have been altered to accommodate his large family plus servants.

The group of houses called today, the Cottage, the Glen, the Manor and the Abbey along with the land called Westley Park, are inextricably linked with related owners and occupants. It becomes very confusing to separate them at their beginning, without looking at the deeds.

Occupants/Owners?

1830 John Tuder to 1836 approx. (not certain).

1831 Mrs Mary Robson relict of R. Robson of Doncaster and her daughters Jane, and Theodosia, who constructed a fernery in the chapel ruins.

1873 The Rev. John James Smith of Norfolk with 5 servants.

1892 John Broughton Lambert.

1900 T. D. Cunningham.

1911 John Power was in residence. He wrote to the Church Commission requesting them to sell part of a field adjoining the Abbey grounds and the vicarage, in order to make a private drive to the main road. At first the vicar was willing, but later refused on the grounds that he would lose his privacy and be 'overlooked'. This was in 1912 and permission was never given.

There was a valuation of the Abbey, Westly Park and The Glen by T. Rule Owen on 18th Feb. 1914.

1923 William Belingham Jameson (the Whisky distillers).

19?? Col. Morgan James Saurin.

1932 Major Mark Saurin.

1945 Captain Augustine E. L. James (his son was killed at Arnhem).

1957 Ivor and Gwyneth Evans (brother to Laurie Evans at Court Farm).

1968 The Frobels.
1975 Major Dewson.
1985 G. & E. Warren who also owned The Cottage after 1991.

This rough sketch of the device on the Abbey wall represents two five pointed stars, a rose, and a tree, on a shield.
The Bosanquet family heraldic device is exactly the same, save for a crescent instead of a rose, and with quartering.

Juniper Cottage (illustrated) circa 19th century. There was another cottage alongside this one. Originally No. 1 & 2 St Teilo Cottages. They may well have been early 18th century. Unfortunately, it cannot be clearly seen, but the lady leaning against the wall is wearing the traditional high beaver hat that welsh women wore up to the mid-19th century.

The brothers Morris lived in both these cottages with their families in the 1880's, they were both Blacksmiths. It is possible there was a cottage similar to these, on the North side of the church, foundations are just visible in dry weather. In the background of this picture you can see what was originally the front of Court Villa (Giltar Lodge).

Next we see the row of houses behind the church. Whitehouse is unseen left, then Rock Villa, **Myrtle Cottage** (the old Post office) and **White Rock**. These two last mentioned, are likely late Georgian. It is just possible to make out the signboard on Myrtle house.

These cottages were originally a part of the Cooke Estate as was Penally House, and when Clement Williams owned the Manor, he persuaded all of them to give up 16 feet of their gardens, with the promise of a back entrance if required. This arrangement enabled him to have easier access to Penally House by horse and carriage.

Both illustrations from collection of Leslie Edwards.

Penally had its own franking system, and Postal deliveries were twice a day.

Circa 1835? – **The Cross Inn**, was a pair of cottages originally, placed at the western end of this row. Leslie Edwards, who still lives at Rock Villa, tells me his mother was born in one of them, and the family held both.

Combined they became the Cross Inn, and in 1888 were leased to James Williams, the Narberth Wine Merchants. Again owned by the Cooke Estate, the freehold was purchased in 1927. The Cross Inn, has been the subject for many visiting artists, and has been used to illustrate a

Cross Inn, Penally.

calendar by Reeves, the local publishers, who once lived in the village at The Cedars.

Hoskins' map of 1842 marks buildings but does not name them.

A house at Daniel Leys existed which is possibly the foundation of Highlights. So did Red House and a cottage just west of the Wheelabout called Ridgeway, which is now a total ruin. Rose Cottage existed, but not Hill cottages in front of it, they came after the Army camp was established. Other than these, I believe Fern House replaced an earlier cottage. Of course by this time all the farmhouses were built, and they too had a number of buildings marked on each, some of which were dwellings.

There was a house in the position of Lydstep Mansion on the shore, built by the Adams family in the middle Georgian period.

There is little documentary evidence to be exact, but I think it likely that Bower Cottages, Alma Cottage, two others on the Ridgeway next to the boundary, a group at Frankleston, Duck's Puddle (Common Hay) a group at Middle Walls and two called Hoill, and Court Cottage, were in existence before 1842.

Analysing the Census for 1841, I counted 31 houses in what was the village at that time. There were 28 farms, which totalled 37 dwellings if one included their out-buildings, which brings the grand total of 68 dwellings in the whole parish. So few houses were built over a 100 years period, it was an event that everyone watched with interest.

To summarise this view of the village before the industrial revolution, it will be obvious that agriculture was still the main employer, and the seasons, still the clock that people lived by and understood.

But all this was about to change.

A top hat was even worn for gardening as seen in J. C. Loudon's Magazine 1832, which recommends mowing in an advertisement as an ideal recreation for a Gentleman.

Finally, the following extract (page 88) from a *Tenby Observer* news-copy of the 1950's tells a sad story of the time. Unfortunately, the stone no longer exists.

In the church register, William Thomas of Tenby aged 37, and Thomas Thomas aged 45, are recorded for that date, although Ann Thomas was the only one recorded on the stone.

Other burials took place in surrounding parish churches.

A CHRISTMAS EVE TRAGEDY OF OVER 100 YEARS AGO

By Arthur L. Leach

IN the burial ground and facing towards the west door of Penally Church stands a gravestone commemorating a tragedy, one which was, perhaps, the greatest known local disaster.

More than a century's winds, rains and frosts have obliterated much of the memorial inscription leaving only these fragments :—

....
.... THOMAS
drowned with Twen ....
between Tenby and Caldy ....
.... December 27th, 183...

Forty years ago, more of the lettering being then readable, the personal name could be read as " ANN THOMAS " and, unless my memory is at fault, one line mentioned Giltar Sands as the place where the body was washed ashore.

It would appear from this inscription that twenty persons, at least, lost their lives on December 27th but, in the only printed account of the accident known to me, viz. p. 67 of Miss Bourne's "Guide to Tenby," 1843, the number given is 17 and the year is 1836. The date " December 27th " which differs from Miss Bourne's " Christmas Eve," may be that on which the body was recovered.

Miss Bourne's account, written only a few years after the tragic occurrence, is likely to be correct ; the gravestone may not have been set up until many years later when details were less well remembered.

Accepting Miss Bourne's words and adding some few particulars of general interest, the story of what happened on that stormy Christmas Eve 118 years ago may be briefly told.

ADVICE IGNORED

In 1836, when many quarrymen and labourers were working on the limestone cliffs at Eel Point near the western end of Caldey, a party of seventeen men and women planned to sail to Tenby on Christmas Eve to spend the festive season with relatives and friends in the town.

On the appointed day a furious wind, blowing from the west, roused the sea to such terrible violence that Mr. Cabot Kynaston, owner of the island, urged the party not to attempt to cross to the mainland.

His advice was disregarded ; the ill-fated boat, one of Tenby's luggers, set sail and was soon plunging in the billows which raced across the roadstead.

She ploughed her way safely, if dangerously, through the angry waters until she was passing the Sker Rock, a little to the south-east of St. Catherine's Rock. Then a great wave overwhelmed and overturned her.

She sank within sight of many anxious townsfolk gathered on Castle Hill to watch her perilous passage from Caldey ; all on board were drowned.

Bodies were cast ashore at various points along the coast and given burial but the only known grave is that of Ann Thomas who, after that wild and disastrous crossing, found a resting-place in Penally's quiet churchyard.

Chapter 4

Victorian Penally, 1837-1901

WITH THE CROWNING of the young Queen Victoria, we take a great leap forward in the matter of education, morality and the importance of the family.

All over the country, populations were on the move to the new industrial areas, and villages were in decline. It was quite a different story in Penally, this miniature Georgian village was actually growing. The introduction of the Census in 1841 and those of following decades, show this growth clearly, as the increase in different work activity reached its peak in the following 50 years.

The minor gentry, such as ex-East India Company people, retired Service personnel, Church dignitaries and professional classes, favoured this beautiful spot as a place in which to live. Penally and Tenby had become the watering places where genteel families chose to spend their summer.

By 1861 there were three times as many houses in the parish and by 1871 the population had doubled.

Penally Manor.[1] Listed Grade 2 by CADW.

The Villa was designed by the architect James Harrison in 1839 and exhibited at the Royal Academy He was commissioned by Charles Cook Wells who owned the land. Like the Abbey it is an example of the battle of architectural styles that existed right through Victorian times. The Cooke estate also owned Westley Park the land on which the Glen was built. Charles Cooke Wells's son, Hugh, was born in Penally in 1844.[2]

---

1. The photograph (on page 90) was kindly lent by Mrs Brenda Evans of Bubbleton who was Brenda Callingham when she lived there after WW2.
2. Information from Thomas Lewis, *A Dictionary of British Architects, 1600-1840*.

Penally Manor.

It was first called **Cooks Villa** in Pigot's Directory of 1844, an understandable choice of name in consideration of its benefactor.

Occupants were:

1840/50 Charles Cook Wells.
1851   Chas C Wells pew in church for Penally House but 1851 Census shows W. I. Knight gent. of London, with 3 servants.
1852   Nicholas Dunn Esq?
1859   Henry Mathias of Haverfordwest who later went to Trefloyne.
1859   Power of Attorney: To take admittance of Penally House in the village and a house and two gardens in the village.
           1. Reverend Richard Brooke of York. Clerk.
           2. Chas Cook Wells of the village and parish 30 Sept. 1859 surrendered by Henry Mathias of H'west gent, 4th May 1860.

1871 Charles Hugh Brown Wells, Solicitor (Son).
1880 William J. O. Holmes Esq, from Norfolk, with 5 servants. There was a valuation done in 1884 when it was proposed the Manor be enfranchised.
1889 John Forbes.
1890 Clement John Williams. 6 times Mayor of Tenby and patron of the Village. He bought the Old Palace garden and a field near the Barracks at this time for £400.
1912 Sir David Hughes-Morgan Bart: Edwin Duffy at the Lodge was his chauffeur. Draft Conveyance of 1914 for Penally House & The Glen and a field called Westly Park consideration £150.
  1. Sir C. E. G. Philipps.
  2. Morgan James Saurin of Orielton, Col.
  3. Geo Fisher of York.
  4. Constance Mari York Schofield and Rev. James Schofield of Cornwall.
1945 Charles H. Callingham. His widow still lives in the village.

The end of the Georgian period and the beginning of the Victorian, overlap to some extent. Ordinary dwelling houses stand astride both periods if they have no specific architectural feature. Smaller houses like Alma Cottage also span the periods. The County is not famous for its wealth of domestic architecture, so it is all the more surprising to find, in this one village, so many of late Georgian, Romantic and early Victorian examples. They were to be followed later by a preference for bungalows and verandahs through the colonial influence.

The Glen. It was built by Benjamin Phillips on earlier foundations in 1851. The building of it led to a Court case when it was finished between Phillips and Miss Theodosia Robson, over an excess in the estimate. It was advertised in the *Tenby Observer* viz:

 1855 TO LET, unfurnished, with 5 bedrooms, a coachouse, etc.
 1861 Richard Welsley Army Surgeon.
 1864 Charles Buttingham Gent rented.
 1865 Edmund Southey Gent lived there with his wife Alice.

1886   Sir William Seton.
1923   Edith Barnes.
1955   Margaretta Watson.

Fern House, was built over Fern Cottage on land owned by Charles Mathias possibly around the 1870's. It was occupied by the Mathias family at the end of the century, and in 1888 Henry Hugh Mathias the Surgeon, was born there. He was the youngest brother of Dr Charlie with whom he shared a surgery later in life. His father died the year he was born and is buried in Penally.

Regrettably, lots of the properties were not named on electoral lists or census returns, or named differently. For example, Corse cottages numbered 1, 2, 3, & 4 in a row, next to the Crown Inn.

No's 1 & 2 of the Terrace existed before 1881, and two more were being built that year. There were three houses on 'the commons' numbered 1, 2, & 2, the last one occupied by the village policeman Benjamin Evans. Two families were still living in No's 1 & 2 The Old Palace in Lydstep as late as 1880, which now appears to have been a ruin for ages. Little Crackwell was called Out of Sight, and Bubbleton Green was known as The Laundry.

We can see which houses existed by the turn of the century on this O.S. map (opposite). Unfortunately, there is no earlier map of the same scale and detail.

However, staying with the beginning of Victoria's reign the earliest population Census gave only brief information. It was difficult to read in places, and did not refer to individual houses, but we do get a glimpse of family names in the 40 dwellings the enumerator Benjamin Edwards found on the night of **April 1st 1841**.

Heads of family only

Charles Edwards	John Evans	Sophia?	Ann Harris
Mary Andrews (Cay)	Mary Davies	Wm Skirme	James Harris
George Evans	Griffith Evans	David Rees	John Skirme
Thos Evans	Ed Davies	Emanuel Davies	James Morris
George Beddows	Barbara Bois (Ind)		Hannah Davies
Mgt Davies	Agnes Dynchy? (Ind)		Wm Barns (Ind)

Victorian Penally, 1837-1901

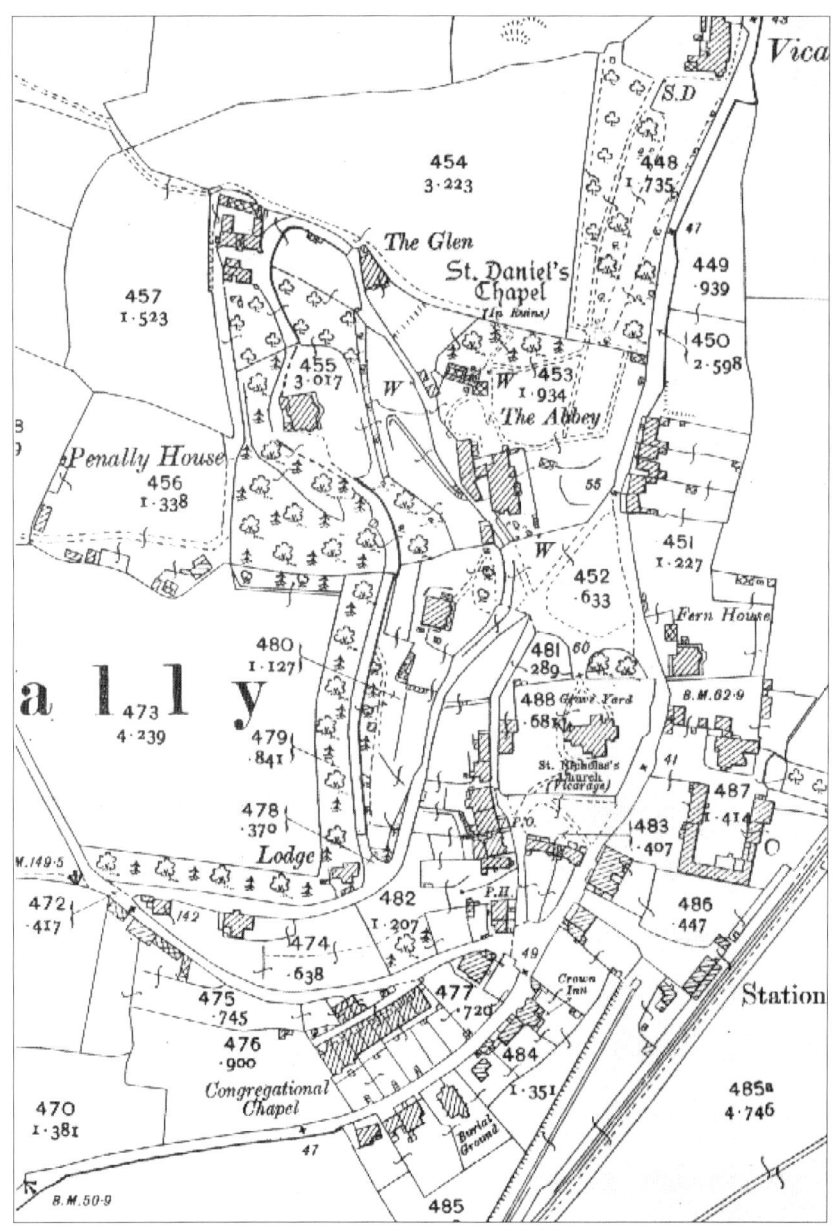

O.S. map of the Village 1907.

John Skirme (Common House)		Mary Skirme (Park Ho)
Sarah John (Hoill)		Wm Davies (Hoill)
John Adams (Old Pound)		John Griffiths (Ridgeway Ho)
John Llewelyn (Oxland)		John Davies (Wheelabout)
Mark Waters (Daniels Ley)		John Morgan (Red Ho)
Wm Morris (Mid Walls)		John Griffith
Richard Morris	Thos John	Wm Edwards (W. Holloway)
John Davies	Wm Harris	John Hughes, Minister.

We also know their occupations, for example: there was a blacksmith with 2 apprentices, a schoolmaster, 4 shipwrights with 5 apprentices, 2 carpenters/joiners and their apprentices, 2 shoemakers, 3 masons, 3 seamstresses and 11 farmworkers with their families.

By the time of the next Census in 1851 however, there were 81 dwellings which included 6 gentry and 2 landed proprietors, with 35 house servants between them. Domestic Service was becoming an attractive alternative to farm work.

We can deduce that most of the new building in the village took place in earnest between 1850 and 1870 and continued to the turn of the century.

We can tell where some of these names lived by the Tithe record for the following year. Tithes were the tax farmers had to pay to support the parish church and the clergy. Always a contentious tax, they were obliged in earlier times, to give one tenth of their annual produce, in kind. Tithe Barns were built to house this payment, in kind.

The Act of 1836 replaced this type of payment with a tithe-rent charge. A survey was required to provide accurate land measurement and cultivation records. Thus we get a splendidly detailed record not only of the owners and occupiers, but the field names and numbers, as well as some idea of the layout and buildings of each farm from the tithe maps.

1842 Tithes

Farm	Owner		Occupier
Hill	Thos Waters	51a	George Hughes
New House	Thos Winch	11a	Joseph John

Farm	Owner		Occupier
The Mount	Mark Waters	2a	Mark Waters
Drusselton	Sir R. Philipps		Frank Beddoe
Vicarage land	Rev. J. Hughes	173a	Rev. Hughes
Pepper Park	Martha Cook	2a	David Beddoe
Beaconny Hills	J. Sinnet Griffith	16a	J. S. Griffith
Court Ho Farm	Sir R. B. Philipps		Robert Waters
& part Trefloyne			
Robertswalls	ditto		George Williams
Marsh Bridge	ditto		Elizabeth Brown
Great Tarr	ditto		Eliz. Llewhelin
West Tarr	ditto		John Gwyther
Palmers Lake	ditto		Wm Rogers
Crackwell	Chas Cooke Wells	209a	James Millard
Whitewell	ditto		Martha Beddoe
and other lands about			Thos Williams
			Martha Llewhelin
			Mary Skyrme
			John Davies
			C. C. Wells
Holloway	Chas Mathias	313a	Arthur Williams
Marsh	ditto		C. Mathias
Trefloyne	Sir R.B.P		Robert Waters
Lidstup	Ann Barlow	261a	James Parcell
part W. Bubbleton	John Adams	61a	Margaret Smith
Carswell	Charity land	95a	James Hughes
Bubbleton	Sir R.B.P		William Smith
	George Scale	4a	
other parts	John Tudor	2a	
	George Williams	13a	& John Wilkinson

In the last quarter of the 19th century the Steward of the manor still held Courts in Manorbier and Penally, notice was given in the local press and the jurors were entertained to dinner. The law of copyhold was not abolished until 1922.

The largest landowners on the 1842 Tithe were:

Sir Richard Bulkley Philipps with 1134 acres (Trefloyne).
Charles Mathias with 313 acres of marshland.
Charles Cooke Wells with 240 + 11acres of glebe land, (?) the largest private landowner.

But there were also large tenant farmers like James Parcell with 320 acres and 8 labourers, and Robert Waters with 600 acres and 10 labourers. Along with the Vicar, such men would have held great sway in local affairs.

Many agricultural workers now lived away from the farms they worked. It is noticeable too, that the population in the 1851 Census was drawn from many parts of the country outside Wales. As both the Army Camp and the Railway developed, so houses were built for their special needs, like Crossing cottage, the Station Masters house, Railway Inn, Kiln House Blackrock Cottage, for quarry business, Starvation (Hill houses) for the Army interest, some houses on Giltar Terrace, Court Villa, for expected visitors,the Chapel and Glanymor for the new chapel Pastor.

Leaders sprang up in the community that were not automatically the landowners, as in the past, but strong men with vision and conviction. Men like John Morgan Griffiths who led the way in farming and founded the Non-Conformist Chapel, and David Davies of Llandinam the entrepreneur and dynamo of the Tenby Pembroke Railway, who changed everyone's way of travel and supply. The War Department had cast its eye on Penally too, and was to have a profound impact on this small village.

Dealing with each huge change to the way of life in Victorian Penally, I shall give an account of each, separately, although they all happened at much the same time.

Education
As we have seen, Penally school started in 1786 with an unknown Schoolmistress, who gave up in 1824 because she was 'very old'. William Owen was the next we know about.

Pembrokeshire's schools were poor financially, and most came in for scathing reports from the Commissioners, particularly in the Welsh speaking areas. Only Cresselly and Castlemartin had any praise. Most of the teachers were incompetent and the buildings were often in a poor state of repair.

They offered at best a very basic education, and parents were not convinced time spent at school was of any benefit, when the child could be earning money in the field. Here is the result of the enquiry into Penally school:

1846
Commissioners Enquiry into the state of Education in Wales

"The schoolroom has been built by the vicar Rev. J. Hughes, on ecclesiastical ruins. The walls are sound, but the floor, the roof, and one of the windows are out of repair. The master writes well with his left hand, having lost, when young, the use of his right hand. He said 'I teaches' several times.

The major part of the scholars are labourers and mechanic's children, who pay 1d a week. The sum of £13 is guaranteed to the master by the vicar, which is made up by subscriptions and a collection in church. The girls are taught sewing by Mrs Bough Allen, and the rest by a woman paid by Miss Jane Robson (who lived at the Abbey).

The 14th chapter of Romans was read, and to questions proposed by me (the master was engaged in receiving money towards the clothes club) they said that Paul wrote this Epistle – did not know what Epistle meant, nor what was Paul's original name – he persecuted the church – knew nothing of his conversion, nor where Rome was.

Pembroke is bounded on the east by Carmarthenshire, on the south by the Bristol Channel, on the west by the Irish Channel – did not know by what it was bounded on the north – did not know the countries composing Great Britain.

Seven days in a week, twelve months in a year, named them correctly with the number of days in each month.

In arithmetic: 7 x 7 = 49, 8 x 4 = 32, 6 x 4 = 24, 16oz in a pound, 20cwt in a ton, 1700 yards in a mile, 6s 8d = ⅓ of a pound, 5s = ¼ of a pound 7s = ⅓ of a guinea, divide 661 by 51, and worked as 1 lb 3 and ¾. 24 and ¾lb and 5678 at 6 and ½ (by practice) correctly. Some of the copybooks were fairly written.

20 boys and 10 girls attend.

G. B. Hughes informed me that the labourer's wages on their own finding are 1s 2d a day, masons and carpenters get 2s or 2s 2d or 2s 6d.

Farm servants from £4 to £8 a year (they do not attend the Sunday school and there is no evening school in the parish) female servants 50s to £4 a year.

He knew of no drunkards in the parish. There was only one public house, and very little business was done in that. Farmers could read and write, so could labourers also who were brought up in the parish in the last 25 years, but imperfectly.

The people are steady and very industrious."

Signed by *William Morris*
29th December 1846.

The Schoolmaster at this time was William Owens who was 60 years old, and lived at Frankleston.

The school struggled on for another nine years before an application was made in 1855 by the parishioners of Penally to the Poor Law Guardians for permission to purchase the dilapidated building in order to rebuild it as a house for the schoolmaster. The guardians ultimately gave the building to the parish, the value of it at the time was NIL, and so it became the schoolmasters house, and the old building at its rear was altered to serve as the new school. In 1860, 21-year-old William Smith from Tetbury in Gloucester was appointed Master. He remained for 14 years and would have seen the exciting move to a brand new village school.

Queen Victoria once said that education was ruining the working class, making them unfit for work as servants and labourers. Shocking to our ears now, but this was the general attitude and anxiety felt by many in power. There was no enthusiasm to improve the chances of a good education for all children until almost twenty years later.

At a vestry held in the schoolroom, 'after due notice given this 21st day of December 1871, for electing a committee of five persons to direct and superintend measures for building a new school in the Parish of Penally, the undernamed persons were proposed and elected':

John Hughes . . . . Chairman (the vicar)
Captain Walls?
Francis Watt, Esq
James Parcell . . . .
Robert Parcell . . . . . . Churchwardens

The school cost £339.00 to build. It was opened on August 25th 1873. Officially, sixty children of both sexes were instructed, supported by an annual subscription of £52.14.00 on average, described as 'expenditure for support of the poor'.

The original schoolroom became a Reading room for the men of the village and material for this was supplied by the church and others in the village.

The Admittance Register shows, on its first two pages, the children that attended in that year. It is written in the most beautiful 'copper-plate' hand, presumably by William Smith, Headmaster. No longer a church school it was now under Government Inspection.

The school committee decided 'a mistress would be able to manage it instead of a master' (no doubt it was a good deal cheaper too) and in 1873 they appointed Mrs Sarah Parrett, as Headmistress. There is a memorial to her 'devoted work among the children of the parish' which villagers placed on the pulpit in the church in 1880 although she only served 5 years.

There was an unhappy succession of Pupil Teachers, who lasted a very short time according to the school Log Book which makes fascinating reading. Some only lasted a month. There are constant Inspectors reports, and visits by the local gentry and the vicar. Generally one gets the feeling of a heavy well-meaning oppression.

School attendance fluctuated with the seasons, the harvesting and planting, and extremes of weather. Little children had so far to walk from outlying farms on the extremes of the parish boundary, the school simply closed in bad weather. Often the reports are about drying children off before they could be sent home again.

Epidemics of whooping cough, measles and scarlet fever, through the wintertime especially, closed the school for three or four months. There were days off for funerals, which were frequent, and a short break of 3 weeks for summer taken in June.

In March 1886, 52 of the children had measles. The Reverend Morris looked in, and decided it should close for a further week because 'some of the little ones seem very much weakened. Several have bad eyes and many are deaf.' Six more cases followed, and three more in September. Muriel

Davies, Annie Grey and Elizabeth Griffiths, William Hughes and Fred John stayed away with bad eyes, and John Williams and Hannah Hughes died in October.

The early years of the life of the school make sad reading. Hardly a winter passed without an epidemic of some contagious disease playing havoc with the numbers of children actually learning anything at all. Isolation was not practiced, so this miserable state of affairs continued year after year.

There was relief when in the new year of 1887 Mary Pullin took over as Headmistress, she was to serve in that capacity for forty good years.

Penally School 1894.

This early picture was copied from the original held by Mrs Gwladys Evans. Gwladys is the niece of Emma James, who is standing 5th left at the back, but she could not identify any of the other children. Both Emma and her sister Alice became pupil teachers at the school. Mary Pullin the Headmistress, is sitting in the middle of the picture, she finally resigned in 1929.

Until she joined the school there was no syllabus of subjects taught, and the boys in particular were very unruly. Apart from all this, the school was severely handicapped by the lack of paper, pens, ink and desks. The main accomplishment seems to have been 'singing' and in this the children excelled. The choir attended most funerals. The local 'gentry' made frequent visits to hear them sing.

Ladies in the village like Mrs Watts, Mrs Voyle and Miss Clifton instructed the girls in needlework, and the Barrack Sergeant drilled the boys for an hour once a week.

There is a long list of pupil teachers over the years, they attended their own educational classes at the Intermediate School (with mixed results) during the time they were pupil teaching.

In 1881, one of them, Florence Hall, was dismissed 'for keeping low company'. In the period of stability that followed when Miss Pullin took charge, there were glowing reports from the HMI Diocesan Inspector who found she taught clearly and intelligently.

Unfortunately, when she took time out to marry, her replacement, Catherine Painter Venables was not able to maintain discipline or improve school work, so the school received no grant that year. Normality returned when Mary came back as Mrs Osborne and there was a big effort made to improve attendance and quell the unruly!

Throughout the next two years discipline was metered out in the struggle to return to order. John Evans in particular seems to have been consistently naughty, and his brother William was not much better.

School attendance was the other problem Mrs Osborne tackled, along with the help of the attendance officer and bribes from Clement Williams. However, the children were allowed to gather mushrooms and taken to village weddings, so school life was not all doom and gloom.

In 1891 there was free education.

On July 1st 1896 the school was closed for the funeral of two relatives of the James family. They were John James, who ran the shop, and his son John Henry James; both had drowned in a current off Giltar. The 17 year old son had been a pupil at the school and Emma James in the school photograph, would have been his sister.

When it first opened the school measured 39ft by 18ft. The only classroom was 20ft by 16ft and it was 13ft high. There was a stove to heat the room, and the children were called by a bell.

Religion

After the Rev. John Hughes 'reconstruction' of St Nicholas, the new gallery could accommodate sixty more souls, and now there could be an allocation of pews to the more important in the village.

Upright Victorians were mightily aware of the order of things, and the pews in the church were strictly 'appropriated'.

In 1851 the allocation was as follows:

Pew No:
1. Parcell of Lydstep
2. Parcell
3. Vicar
4. Wm Smyth of Holloway
5. " And Bubbleton
6. Charles C. Wells Penally House
7. Whitewell and Crackwell
8. Gwyther of Tarr
9. David Rees. Roberts Wall
10 Robsons for both houses
11. Mark Waters of Hill
12. Palmers Lake/ Little Bubbleton

13. Joseph Johns New House
14. Waters of Trefloyne
15. Clerk's seat
16. Waters of Court Farm
17. Bond of Churchill
18. Llewhellin of Tarr
19. Ditto
20. Waters of Holloway
21. Charles Edwards House
22. Waters of Penholloway
23. Dorothy/John Beddoes
24. James Griffiths Houses

The rest are 'freely' open.

The Church Book for 1835 shows fixed annual payments to Morgan the Clerk of £4. Morris for organ blowing £2. Skyrme care of yard £5. Watkins care of church £4. Insurance £1.3.9.

Other payments were for journeys to Pembroke 2/6 – and Haverford-west 9/6. The largest sums paid were for repairs to the church by Charles Edwards £3.17.7. – and Mr Kummans bill for wine £1.17.4.

In 1857, a deeply religious man called John Morgan Griffiths, arrived at Court Farm. He was 6'3" tall, broad shouldered, with dark hair, and a fast talker. Born in Llanglydwen, Carmarthenshire in 1834. A great Temperance man and a Liberal, he worshipped at St Florence Congregational church, which had been founded by his grandfather.

From the turn of the century, Nonconformist ministers had been visiting the area, preaching at Bubbleton, Whitewell, Drussleton, Holloway and Frankleston. In 1856 the Congregational churches were used alternatively once a month at St Florence, Manorbier Newton, Bubbleton and Court Farm.

When, in 1863, the railway was being constructed, workmen from all over the country came to reside in the area, and they began to use the railway blacksmith's hut at Drusselton bridge for services on a Sunday. John started a Sunday School for children in the store-loft of Penally Court, and then in the barn, which continued for 20 years.

Then in 1886 a copyhold cottage was bought at auction for £100, it must have been one of the Corse Cottages, and a building committee was formed. John Morgan Griffiths was the driving force behind the organising and building of the United Reform Church, which opened with its first service in 1887. The building seated 150 adults or 200 children. He was the first Pastor.

John Griffiths had taken on Court Farm when he was only 23 years old, it amounted to 440 acres and gave employment to 3 men and 2 boys. The landlord had built a 'commodious' house for him on the site where the old Court Leet was held, and he lived there with his wife Anna, their two sons, four daughters and two housemaids.

Described as a 'gentleman farmer', he was certainly a progressive one, and represented the Welsh tenant farmer on the Royal Commission on Land question in Wales.

Miss Mary Griffiths demonstrating her butter making in the service of Queen Victoria.

He was also a member of the Parish Council, a member of the Technical Education Committee, Agricultural correspondent for Pembs Board of Agriculture, Founder and Vice-Chairman Pembs Farmer's Club, and the first Welshman to adjudicate at Smithfield Show as breeder of Welsh Black cattle.

His daughter Mary, lectured on dairy farming and was four years superintendent of the late Queen Victoria's dairy at Balmoral Castle, his daughter Elizabeth played the organ.

At his death in 1904, the sale of his stock attracted over 800 people, who lunched at Penally Court.

There is a biography, with an appreciation by Lord Carrington of Gwydyr Castle and other eminent men, published in 1905.

Court Farm was greatly affected by the arrival of the railway. The disruption of the roadway through to the beach, the decimation of some farm buildings, and in other more dramatic ways, as reported in the *Tenby Observer* of January 23rd 1896, quote:

THE PENALLY FATALITY

In connection with the Penally fatality which occurred on the level crossing last August causing the death of William Morgan, a farm labourer in the employ of J. M. Griffiths of Penally Court. An appeal made in the *Tenby Observer* in the names of J. M. Griffith and F. B. Mason Trustees, raised £110. unquote.

The headstone at St Nicholas where he was buried reads:

In loving memory of
William Morgan
Who was accidentally killed on Railway Crossing
Aged 83 years.

Imagine, he was still working at that age!

Meadow Cottage was built with the money and widow Morgan moved in, paying a ground rent of 5/- per annum on lease for 99 years, granted by Sir Charles Philipps. Today, it has been renamed Kingfisher Cottage, it is next to the Post Office.

At the church, David Melville Morris succeeded the Reverend Hughes in 1873. Like John Griffiths, he was also a young man of 28 years when he took up his position. Though he lived at the Vicarage, he also farmed 130 acres and employed 2 men and a boy. He and his wife Isabella had no children of their own, but a stepdaughter, Ethel de N. Clifton. They kept 2 servants.

One of these was a William Morris who lies buried at St Nicholas, 'faithful servant at the vicarage for 55 years', died 1900, aged 88. A loyal servant indeed!

The Reverend Morris inspired loyalty in his church also. His Verger Thomas Morgan had come to live in the village in 1883.[3]

He was a deeply religious young man of 26 years, living at Frankleston Cottage with his wife Martha. They had three children already, and a further nine were born at Middlewalls. All twelve children did well, but only Cissie and Fred, the youngest, lived their lives out in Penally.

Thomas became the village carpenter, and his grandaughter Doris would often say how she remembered him, busy in his workshop, curly pieces of wood shavings dropping from his plane. Sometimes she would watch him etching in his beautiful copperplate handwriting, the nameplate for an ordered coffin.

As undertaker and gravedigger he served the village folk, until his death in 1923. Martha, his wife, died five years later, and was survived by eight sons and two daughters, all married.

Of the children, Mary worked at Lydstep Haven for Lord St Davids and married his chauffeur. Albert was a master Tailor and worked for Weatherall Ltd bespoke tailors to the military and hunting world. Howie was a signalman on the great Western Railway. Stanley went to America, William joined the Merchant Navy, Cissie lived out her life in Penally, as did Fred.

This youngest son, Fred Morgan (1899-1957), followed his father in the task of caring for the dead of the parish, except for the years during the war when he served in the Dragoon Guards.

Fred Morgan and first-born.

3. Notes from Tom's great grandchild, Jennifer Ball.

Billhead by kind permission of George Cavil.

Between father and son, they covered 100 years of 'undertaking' to the parish and service to the church. Fred was also one of the bellringers along with Jo Joseph of Giltar Farm, Jimbo Morris and Ted Rose of the Cross Inn.

Fred and his wife Bessie lived at Middlewalls prior to building a bungalow called 'Ambleside'.

Returning to the Rev. Melville Morris, he was responsible for another major 'restoration' of St Nicholas in 1884 when the unfortunate gallery was removed and other extensive modifications made to the interior.

Five years later during the bitter month of January 1899, there was a fire which might have destroyed the church altogether.

The church was set alight by a faulty heating system that was located beneath the vestry. It was only through the efforts of soldiers from the Connaught Rangers, a great Irish Catholic Regiment stationed at Penally Camp, that the church was saved.

Newspaper accounts describe how 'they were heroically led by the dashing Captain Donoghue who climbed onto the roof, at great risk to himself.' The fire resulted in a great deal of damage, and the vestry was completely destroyed.

Captain Donoghue married the local dressmaker, Alice Griffiths.

An extract from the 'Observer' on January 28th 1899 reads:

> "The Tenby Volunteer Fire Brigade had another opportunity of demonstrating their usefulness in the small hours of Monday morning. In less than an hour after the alarm had been given that Penally church was in danger of being destroyed by fire, the brigade was at work upon the burning building. This is what I call smart work, and equally creditable to officers and men. By the way, I may state, that Dr Lock has resumed his lectures on First Aid to the members of the Brigade."

The Railway

Until 1853 travellers could take a train to Bristol, and continue by sea, after that date, they could train to Carmarthen and take a coach and horses link to Tenby, by 1856 they could train to Neyland and take a ferry crossing to Hobb's Point, but none of these options was simple or convenient.

The opening of the Pembroke to Tenby line was very exciting indeed, it had a huge impact on the whole of the south of the County and Penally in particular. In 1862 two men got together and formed a partnership to construct the Pembroke to Tenby Railway line, all 11 miles, 35 chains of it, for £106,000 in 1862. They were David Davies of Llandinam and Ezra Roberts, although Ezra seems to have been a sleeping partner, and David Davies, a dynamic man and the prime mover.

Work on laying the rail went along smoothly and quickly, but there was difficulty in finding a suitable place to build the station in Penally. The only sizeable earthwork was a long embankment west of the village, thought to be where the remains of an early quayside was found.

This photograph taken in 1905 by the Rev. Connop Price.

A siding was introduced to the existing limestone quarry, greatly increasing business and employment. A small stone hut west of the railway line marks the location of Black Rock junction, although today, it is hard to believe it was ever a junction.

It is overgrown, and the quarry siding is covered by today's huge caravan site known as Kiln Park.

It has been said that heavy plant and material had to be brought by sea, and that Schooners were beached on the South Sands so a roadway was formed across the dunes to the site. Could the roadway have been that used in the earlier centuries, seen on early maps as 'road to Tenby across Whitesands' (South Beach).

When the line was completed in 1864, there were as many as 12 trains a day stopping at the village, and six years later, the Post Office finally agreed to allow the Royal Mail to be carried.

David Davies was an ardent Methodist and would not allow his employees to work on the day of rest, so there were no trains on Sundays though there was a great demand for their use. He brought his own train to the line, called 'Llandinam', after his birthplace in Montgomeryshire, it was the first 'loco' to be used on the new line. All this new construction caused a great stir in the village.

The Railway Inn, seen top left of picture opposite, was built by Henry

James, with stone taken from the quarry below The Mount. The sidings came right up to the back of the Inn and train tickets were sold from there originally.

Henry James and his wife Elizabeth, even had their own beer labels printed, which were never used in fact because the spelling of *Panelly* was incorrect.

Unfortunately, the Inn was not in operation for very long perhaps the rush of visitors did not materialise, so their son John and his wife Margaret changed it to a General Stores.

Tragically, both John and his 17 year old son John Henry, were drowned off Giltar whilst on a fishing trip in 1896.

Seven other children survived. All the girls remained spinsters but one of the boys, Arthur, married Maud from London, and of their two children, Gwladys, has been a wonderful source of local knowledge. John's eldest daughter Mary took the shop over, she was followed in 1917 by her sister Edith, and finally their brother Arthur's daughter.

From Gwladys Evans' collection.

Gwladys Evans, became the proprietor and Post Mistress in 1959. Widowed, she now lives in the house she had converted, that used to be Penally Station.

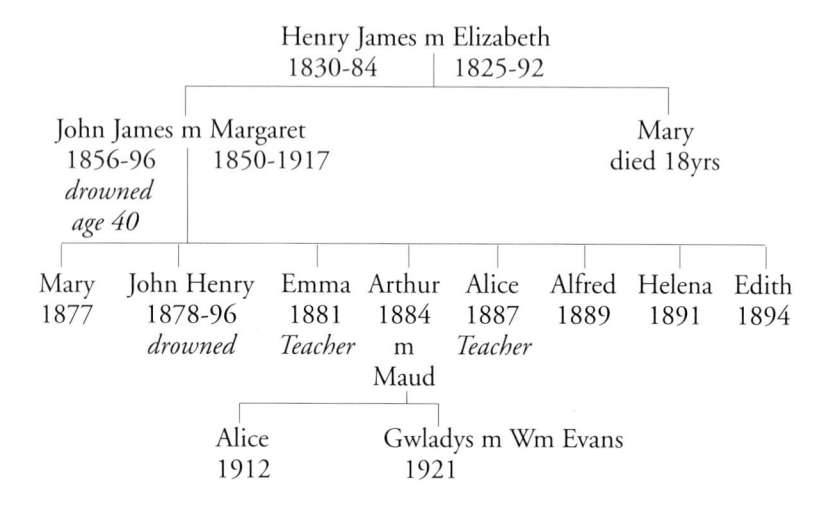

```
                Henry James m Elizabeth
                1830-84    |  1825-92
       ┌───────────────────┴───────────────────┐
John James m Margaret                       Mary
1856-96    | 1850-1917                   died 18yrs
drowned
age 40
   ┌────┬──────┬──────┬──────┬──────┬──────┬──────┐
 Mary  John Henry  Emma  Arthur  Alice  Alfred  Helena  Edith
 1877  1878-96     1881  1884    1887   1889    1891    1894
       drowned    Teacher  m    Teacher
                         Maud
                    ┌─────┴─────┐
                  Alice      Gwladys m Wm Evans
                  1912          1921
```

It is interesting to see how the coming of the railway affected this family over a period of 150 years.

Court Villa was built by the Cooke Estate sometime before the arrival of the railway. All the excitement of the opening of a railway station caused Court Villa, seen in the picture on the left, to move its entrance to face the road to cater for the many new visitors expected. The original entrance facing the church was sealed off with a very nice 'art deco' railing.
Occupants were:

1860 David White, Malster and Brewer of Cosheston. It was willed to his sons John and Richard in 1886.
1894 Captain Pascoe R.N. the leader of the newly formed Parish Council.
1912 Mr Hill-Lowe with his daughter, as well as Lt Colonel R. Wycliffe Thompson DSO, it was then called Giltar Lodge.
1923 Constance Lewis.

1943 Ivor and Gwyneth Evans when it became the **Giltar Lodge** Hotel.

The true benefit of rail travel was seen after the Territorial Army was formed in 1908 when trains brought great numbers of soldiers to Penally to camp, and the station platform was extended to cater for the men, mules, and baggage. Gwladys remembers the excitement and the bustle on these occasions.

Goods trains ran twice a day, easily moving cattle, horses, rabbits etc: to the Markets at Pembroke or Narberth, taking only half an hour, and shop supplies and machinery were brought in. Come to that, it only took 3 minutes for passengers to travel to Tenby.

A Station Master's house was built about 1870. Mr Jones was to be the first and only Master, he must have looked resplendent in his gold braided uniform. He had two porters under him, Cozens and Cavil. Alfred Cozens went on to become Station Master at Lamphey. Later a Mr Williams held the position of signalman at Penally, but was also in charge of the station, though he did not live at the house, nor was he styled the Station Master.

Archie Cavil apparently had an arrangement with Laurie Evans of Court Farm whereby he would blow a whistle to alert him of the train's arrival or departure, that's how personal and caring times were then.

Court Farm was very close to the station and the farm buildings extended through and beyond, before the coming of the railway. The recent by-pass cut through the buildings even more.

The Military

The Penally base was a Musketry Camp.

The origins of this training camp date back to 1858 and unlike most other army camps in the country it was formed as a result of the French Invasion scare after the Crimean War.

The War Department leased 14 acres of land from the Picton Estate in August 1859, in spite of Lady Philipps reluctance to give it up, she resisted even more, when further land was needed in 1909 for a firing range plus a chunk of cliffland for manoeuvers.

In all, it amounted to 220 acres. There were two firing ranges, one of 600 yards nearest the sea and another 100 yards inland. By 1930 the range

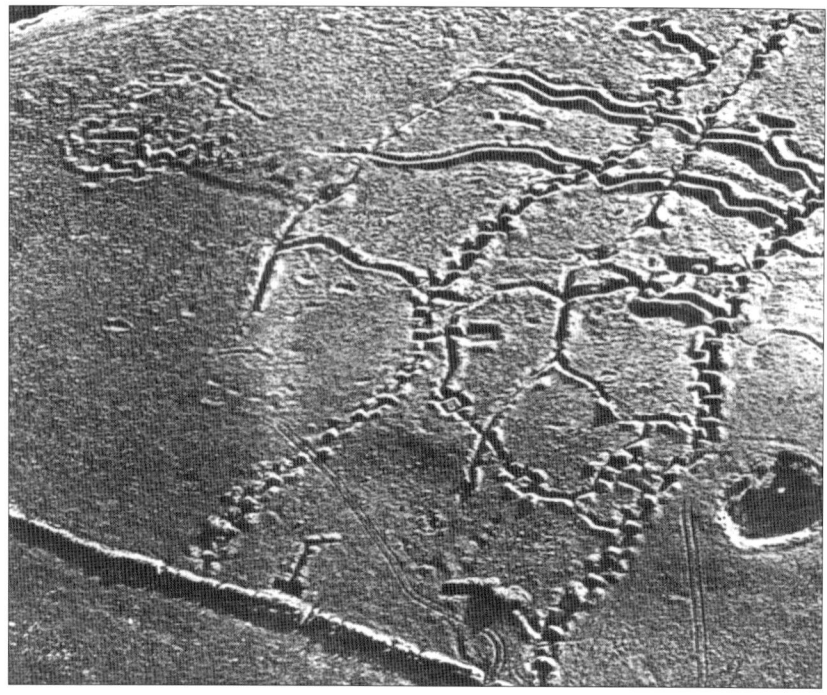

Royal Commission aerial photograph showing WW1 practice trenches still visible today.

by the sea was abandoned. During WW2 there was also a mortar range and a moving target.

Work on Penally Camp finally started in 1860, and was completed a year later. The buildings were all brick with slate rooves. The camp was small at first, and quarters catered for only 4 officers and about 84 soldiers.

The Census of 1871 showed the largest population up to then of 1,080 in Penally, swollen by army men.

Great Britain could never afford a standing army sufficient for her needs and in the early days of the Boer War, Sir Redvers Buller was appealing for 8,000 irregulars 'able to ride decently, but shoot as well as possible.' In October 1899 sanction was given for the formation of 'The Imperial Yeomanry' for service in South Africa.[4]

---

4. From Penally Camp brochure.

Since 1793 the great tradition of the different Yeomanry Companies in this County had been made up of gentlemen and yeomen who supplied their own horses, but now they were being called upon to fight overseas for the first time, and they too trained at Penally. In the summer of 1903 The 3rd Militia Infantry Brigade was doing its Annual Training and 5 Battalions were involved which amounted to 954 soldiers and 19 officers.

This number of soldiers far exceeded the camp's capacity and accommodation had to be provided under canvas. On occasions like these, bell tents and marquees were pitched in the field at Holloway Farm, which is now dissected by the new by-pass, and known to this day as 'Volunteer's Field'. This arrangement was fine during the summer months, but with the outbreak of the First World War, it soon became evident that quartering large numbers of men under canvas during the winter months was not practical.

Penally suffers like the rest of the county with winter storms of wind and lashing rain straight off the Atlantic. So with some urgency in 1915 new barrack huts were set up, which provided an added capacity for 346 men and their officers, but still there was no electricity. Another musketry range was also built to the North of Giltar and a series of practice trenches were dug, the largest of which remains to be seen today, and is a fitting memorial to the men who trained at Penally Camp and lost their lives in the two World Wars.

When they attended church parade at St Nicholas, the soldiers sat on chairs near the altar. Officers and their wives often used rented accommodation, and there were many courtships that ended in marriage, as the parish records show. Many Army children went to the village school, and for a short period, the Barrack sergeant was invited to train all the boys at drill.

The thousands of men that passed through training here inspired many to return years later with their families for holidays or to settle on retirement. It remains one of the most popular camps in Britain.

To celebrate the Jubilee of 1887, Miss Roxon made a gift to the village of the really magnificent water pump that stands below Glanymor and is well cared for. It cost her £70, but put Penally in advance of most other villages, many of which had to wait another 20 years before they had such a luxury. The pump, here illustrated by Geoff Scott of SPARC, was to be the fount of constant deliberation on the newly formed Parish Council for decades, as well as the main source of water.

The Local Government Act of 1888 was to organise rural life and take a lot of pressure off the Church Council.

The same year the Golf Links was established, covering a great deal of the duneland in Penally Parish which belonged to the Mathias family. Fortunately, most of the family were passionate about the game, and when the time came, forty years later, that boundaries were changed, Doctor Charles Mathias was their representative, allowing a seamless transition.

About this time too, sea buckthorn was planted which helped to halt erosion of the dunes.

The Parish Council Act of 1894 followed, and meant that the community governed their own affairs for the first time, by democratic means.

Penally Parish Council held its first meeting that year, in the Schoolhouse, and elected a Chairman in Captain Pascoe RN of Court Villa, proposed by Pearce Griffiths of Trefloyne and seconded by J. M. Griffiths of Court Farm.

Present at the first meeting were:

      1. Edith Barnes   The Glen
      2. John Booth   The Crown Inn
      3. James Waters Brown   Daniels Leys
      4. Marchant Cadwallader Roberts Walls

5. J. W. Griffiths   Penally Court
6. Morgan Griffiths   Penally Court
7. Pearce Llewelyn Griffiths Trefloyne
8. Mike Hackett   Cross Inn
9. Walter Holt   Barrack Master
10. William Jones   Platelayer
11. John Lewis   Minister (Tenby)
12. D. M. Morris   Vicar Penally
13. James T. Parcell   Lydstep
14. John Rogers   Whitewell
15. James Rowlands   Crackwell
16. John Sherring   Labourer, Trefloyn
17. Jo Stubbs   Gardener
18. Clement Williams   Gent: Penally House.

After electing officers and deciding on a bank and meeting dates, they proposed that their first discussion should be Captain Cook's Charity.

The list of recipients to be published in the Reading Room and on the Church door.

Although a great deal was expected of the new parish councils, it was soon discovered, that for all their power, everything they had a mandate to do, was beyond their means. Over the next four years, the minutes record the struggle to supply the school with piped water from the pump, which was going to cost £69. Others could tap into it if they wished at their own expense, plus a contribution to the council.

A survey for this water scheme had cost a guinea, and the Reverend John Lewis, who lived at Glanymor directly above the pump, from the beginning, had been asked to remove his sewage drain from the overflow of the pump.

Later, when it was proposed to pipe water elsewhere in the village. Clement Williams offered to pay £10 to the cost, but in the end he found himself paying £40.

A water committee took responsibility for the success and maintenance of the piping, and in 1898 J. M. Griffiths 'thought the council might congratulate themselves upon the sanitary state of the village. In Penally, they had less sickness than in any of the neighbouring villages.'

The only other business they concerned themselves with, was to enclose 'the green' for which they had consent from Sir Chas Philipps, and they needed a good footpath from the village to Tenby across the burrows, it was satisfactory as far as Black Rock. Mr Rowlands said: 'never mind that, what about the path from the village to Bubbleton bridge for people in winter time.' This comment interests me particularly, because it proves my theory, that the walkway over Crackwell was necessary at that time, to avoid the marsh and flooding of the Alun river in the 18th century.

It served no purpose after tarmacadam arrived, and was so little used that it was completely overgrown and impassable 36 years later. The Rights of Way Act was seen as 'a means of easy trespass' by farmer Rowlands at Crackwell.

However, the path did link the row of houses called Hill Cottages, and Rose Cottage nearby, to the village. They were sometimes called Starvation and were bought by J. M. Griffiths in 1885. Since 1950 they have belonged to Crackwell. There was a clear lane to the farm then and tenants were able to bring their rent over on a Monday, but it is impassable today. Since negotiations with SPARC there is now a style and footpath to the Ridgeway as an alternative to what was a useless 'right of way' ending up in a hedge.

By 1900 Penally Parish Valuation was £3,722.

There seem to have been a great many Reverends and high ranking Naval men living in Penally during these years, many of whom were known to each other. Indeed, many were related or distantly related.

I have found links between the Rowe's, Voyle's, Locks, Saers, Millard's and Skones, and no doubt other seemingly separate arrivals to the village were already friends through the East India connections or the Church.

Before we close this chapter on Victorian Penally, you may find it interesting to know more of some of the important local families.

Charles Cooke Wells

We examined the Cooke family in the last chapter, but Charles Cooke Wells is something of an enigma. He was christened Charles Wells, born in 1800 in Fareham Hants, son of John Wells R.N. He became a Commander in the Royal Indian Navy, and was living in India when Captain Hugh Cook, the illustrious hero, died in 1834.

No WILL was found until Hugh's sister Martha (Patty) Cook discovered it locked in a trunk belonging to him almost a year later.

It named Charles Wells the Executor and sole inheritor of the Cook Estate apart from some bequests to his family and Charities to both Tenby and Penally. Earlier draft WILLS in the keeping of Charles Birt of Tenby, referred to him as 'nephew'.

Miss Martha Cooke, made the necessary noises to get him to return to this country and deal with affairs. She was concerned about the Charity bequests to Tenby and Penally as well as different leases that needed attention.

It was written in the *Tenby Observer* that she insisted Charles add Cook to his name, but there was no mention of that in the codicil.

The inheritance was sizeable and involved large amounts of money in Bonds as well as land and property, for example:

> Penally lands, otherwise known as Cooks Land, also a field called Cook Hays and fields called Barren Park, several cottages, Penally Home Farm, the Post office, 'The Cottage', a public House called the Crown Inn, a cottage, a public House called the Wheelabout, several more cottages also messuages called Bubbleton and Pepper Park.[5]

He also owned Whitewell and land in St Florence and Manorbier.

To this he added properties he reconstructed, plantations of woods he lay down, and new buildings like Court Villa and the Mount.

One could say, that without his influence, Penally would not have attracted the minor gentry to live here, who in turn were large employers and benefactors to the village. For the first time, there were more domestic servants than farm workers living in the village.

His own son, Charles Hugh, was born in Penally in 1844, his daughter Selina was born in Tenby 1842.

He made a WILL in 1855 whilst then living in Brighton, but he did not die until 1888. The Cook Wells estate he eventually bequeathed not to his son, but to his daughter-in-law, Ann Brown Wells in 1883.

---

5. Court Rolls number 324.

He was J.P for the borough of Tenby and Pembroke County. Five times Mayor of Tenby in 1841, 42, 43, 61, and 73 and Vice Admiral of the Port of Milford Haven. He continued a charity to the village to be paid annually to deserving people.

Buried in Penally his tombstone reads:

In memory of Charles Cook Wells late of Penally House
In this parish who died 1882 aged 82 yrs
Also the loved wife of Charles Cook Wells Esq Sophia Annie
Anne Brown wife of Charles Hugh Wells died 1933
Aged 85 yrs cremated Golders Green
Charles Hugh son of Charles Cook Wells died 1902 aged 58 yrs
Buried in Peel Isle of Man.

Clement John Williams
He was a Pin manufacturer and Lithographic printer from Birmingham.

From the time when he took up residence at Penally House, until he died Clement Williams was a great benefactor to the church and to the community. Like all powerful Victorians he enjoyed his position and gave freely of his time and money. He was 6 times Mayor of Tenby and High Sheriff of Pembrokeshire, Alderman and J.P.

The church benefited by the gift of an organ in 1892 which Miss Clifton the Vicar's niece played for the next 50 years. He served on the newly formed Parish Council until his death in 1912. He offered a 'Strawsonizer' for the free use of any local farmer to destroy Charlock or Hadridge.

After his death, the Sales Catologue showed him to be a man of immense property in Tenby as well as bits of land in the parish.

Viz: A skating rink and garage in Picton Terrace. Pleasure gardens in Southcliffe St. 12 dwellings in Bridge St. 1 & 2 Clevedon Cottages. No. 14 the Norton. 11 houses in Greenhill Ave. Ivy Bank House, Rydal nt and Llanfrothen. No. 4 Queens Parade. Newly erected Malvern Lodge plus 8 acres near the barracks, etc. etc.

All publicly auctioned at the Royal Assembly Rooms, Tenby.

His was the first house in the village to be lit by electricity, and he built a Lodge to the 'big house', for his resident electrician. He found time to enjoy a days hunting with Seymour Allen of Cresselly.

He died in 1912, and all the civic dignitaries, local gentry, and many clergy attended his funeral. His pew was draped in black, and covered in flowers. Both Miss Clifton and Mrs Osborne played the organ for the service. He is buried with his wife Katherine, near the Cooke family, although his grave is sadly neglected.

The Voyle family lived at 'The Cottage' for more than a 100 years.
They were one of the long established, respectable, but unlanded families of Pembrokeshire who had close ties with India, but kept their roots in the County.[6]

They pop-up as yeoman farmers in the earliest land tax records, and in 1601 they held Holloway in Penally, and the Landway in Jameston, which they sold to the Scales of Capeston.

There is evidence of Voel's and Voilles in the County even earlier.

However, their rise to prominence starts with William Voyle who married into the Grant family whose influence was essential in helping offspring to get started in India, an impossibility without the recommendation of one of the East Indian Company Directors.

The family owned Norton Cottage in Tenby at the turn of the 19th century, and they used this as a base for their frequent furloughs home, and to raise their families. The sons of these early pioneers, went to Swansea Grammar School and then on to Addiscombe, the E. India. Co. Academy near Croydon. Some of them married in India. Many of the children were born in India, and one or two died there.

When Francis Elliot Voyle died, his wife bought 'The Cottage' in Penally as Norton Cottage had been bequeathed to her stepson. She in turn bequeathed 'The Cottage' to her daughters whilst they were not married, so that her only son Henry, was obliged to live at Bonvilles Court in Saundersfoot on his retirement. The history of the Voyle family is characteristic of many who served in India. Rooted in a sense in Pembrokeshire, they nevertheless spent much of their lives outside it and never actually married anyone from the County.

---

6. Steve Van Dulken, *Pembrokeshire Historical Society*, 1994.

At Easter time this year (2000) a goddaughter of the last surviving Miss Eurith Voyle, called Claire Rendle, deposited a wonderful collection of Voyle family papers with my colleague, Ruth Griffiths.

Amongst the collection are parchments referring to each of the E. India Commissions signed by the different reigning monarchs. Early paintings, portraits, photographs and sillouhettes. Touching letters and descriptions of naval engagements and mutinies. And perhaps most interesting, a handwritten daily account book for the years 1828 to 1831 written by Elliot Voyle, whilst the family were living in Tenby. This must have been Lt. Col. Elliot Voyle who died in 1834. A wonderful record of their daily expenses, the children's allowances, the food that was available, and an insight into life at that time.

I knew Eurith (Urith) very well, we played both golf and bridge together over many years. She did the *Telegraph* Crossword every day, and was mentally very lively, even in her late years. We often played bridge at 'The Cottage' and sometimes at the Abbey where Cynthia Mathias (Dr Charlie's daughter) joined us a few times.

Rumour has it that Eurith worked as a code-breaker during WW2. I can believe it.

Amongst the photographs in the Voyle collection there was one view from 'the cottage' which is a carbon copy of the watercolour by Charles Norris of the ruin that stood there before the house was rebuilt. It would seem to confirm that it is indeed the same site.

The Voyle Family Tree

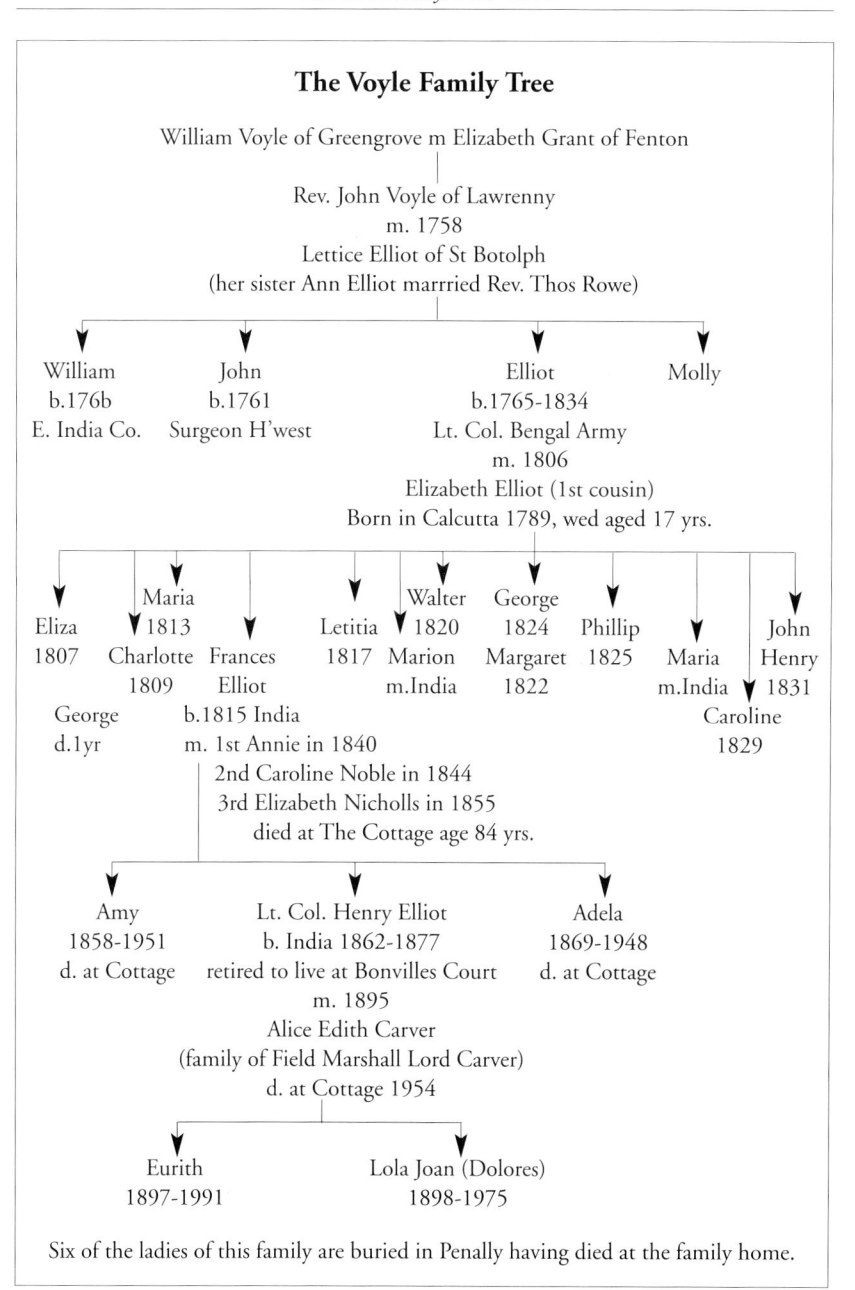

William Voyle of Greengrove m Elizabeth Grant of Fenton

Rev. John Voyle of Lawrenny
m. 1758
Lettice Elliot of St Botolph
(her sister Ann Elliot marrried Rev. Thos Rowe)

William	John	Elliot	Molly
b.176b	b.1761	b.1765-1834	
E. India Co.	Surgeon H'west	Lt. Col. Bengal Army	
		m. 1806	

Elizabeth Elliot (1st cousin)
Born in Calcutta 1789, wed aged 17 yrs.

Eliza	Maria 1813		Letitia	Walter 1820	George 1824	Phillip		John
1807	Charlotte	Frances	1817	Marion	Margaret	1825	Maria	Henry
	1809	Elliot		m.India	1822		m.India	1831
George		b.1815 India					Caroline	
d.1yr		m. 1st Annie in 1840					1829	
		2nd Caroline Noble in 1844						
		3rd Elizabeth Nicholls in 1855						
		died at The Cottage age 84 yrs.						

Amy	Lt. Col. Henry Elliot	Adela
1858-1951	b. India 1862-1877	1869-1948
d. at Cottage	retired to live at Bonvilles Court	d. at Cottage
	m. 1895	
	Alice Edith Carver	
	(family of Field Marshall Lord Carver)	
	d. at Cottage 1954	

Eurith	Lola Joan (Dolores)
1897-1991	1898-1975

Six of the ladies of this family are buried in Penally having died at the family home.

Chapter 5

Edwardian Penally (from 1901)

THE YEAR IS 1901, and Queen Victoria has died. After such a long reign, I thought there would have been some mention of this momentous event in the parish council records, but no, they continued to discuss the state of the water and the need to connect a 2" iron pipe to Alma Cottage. They proposed a 6d rate to defer expenses, 4 voting for, and 5 against. In the end, a tender from Hermann Thomas the 'plumbing' legend of Tenby, was accepted.

The G.W.R. also wanted water and lavatories at the station, for which the parish gave permission, as long as they maintained and paid for the work themselves, and contributed 2 guineas annually to the parish.

However, they did make arrangements to celebrate the Coronation of King Edward VII on June 26th but because of the king's illness, the event was postponed until August 9th when successful athletics and sports were held on the burrows.

In 1903, the parish council sought to preserve the right of way to the beach, over the new rifle range, and C. M. Stokes was paid 5 guineas for negotiating access via the Army.

There had been a complaint that Mr Griffiths at Court Farm was charging a penny every time a cart went through his yard. It was argued that this was a public highway. J. M. Griffiths was offended, saying he only charged for carts taking sand at the request of the Picton Estate. Mr Griffiths died the following year.

The struggle to supply and maintain a water supply continued to occupy the parish over the years. In 1908 water was required to build a few cottages next to the Crown Inn, and it was referred to the newly appointed District Council for approval, as they now had control of building and water supply. Things were looking up.

122

The next year there was a Sunday delivery of post, and this was followed by a proposal to place a chiming clock in the church tower in time for the coronation of King George V. The celebrations were to include, a bonfire at Giltar Head, and sports, ending with a social evening in the schoolroom, Mr Angell to be in charge. He was an exceptionally popular chap, always topping the votes on the council.

Then in 1911 there was an important improvement made to the main road from Holloway bridge and through Yeomanry field, to cut out the dangerous right-angle bend that existed, and a promise to widen the road between the Vicarage and the village.

Lloyd George, then Lord Chancellor, visited the camp in 1912, to present medals to the troops. After inspecting the Yeomanry at Penally Barracks he spent the weekend with Lord and Lady St Davids at Lydstep Mansion. Some suffragettes who were aware of his visit took advantage of the opportunity to cause a disturbance and called Lord St Davids "you traitor" so P.C. Nash of the village was sent for, and ordered to spend the night patrolling the property. The suffragettes would have to wait sometime before their fight was won.

The celebrated and philanthropic C. J. Williams of Penally House, died in 1912. Although some property was changing hands, it was a poor time to sell. His estate was put up for public auction, there were few purchasers, and no bid at all for Penally House or Malvern Lodge. In fact very little was sold.

Eventually, Sir D. J. Hughes-Morgan of the Orielton family, and his wife, Lady Blanche, not only bought the bighouse in 1914, but continued his patronage to the village. The Hughes-Morgans' kept a boat called *The Mary Rose* skippered by Josh Richards and his sons. The boys also crewed *The Bunty* which was owned by the Empress of Abyssinia who had a summer place on Caldey.

Edwin Duffy, was chauffer to the 'big house' and lived at the lodge.

John Power was at the Abbey in 1912, he was unhappy having no access to the main road, so he wrote to the Church Commission requesting them to sell part of the field adjoining the Abbey grounds so that he might make a private drive connecting him to the highway, adding that the vicar was willing. They suggested he should have a right of way rather than buy outright. A month later, however, the vicar changed his mind and refused altogether on the grounds that he might lose his privacy. Mrs Power appears to have leased 'The Cottage' from 1912 to 1918.

The St Davids had done a lot to improve the appearance of the hamlet of Lystep and the building of Lydstep Lodge was highly commended in the local papers.

Lady St Davids was invited to be the parish school manager, she was also nominated to the parish council, but caused a vacancy in 1914 through non-attendance. She was responsible for setting up a Parish Magazine called *Our Village Society Chronicle* which covered interests in Manorbier, Penally, St Florence and Gumfreston.

Hugh Angell was both her editor and secretary on the *Chronicle*, but he left to join the Army in 1914, and Lady St Davids died in 1915. The *Chronicle* ceased shortly afterwards. This was a great pity, since it gave a unique picture of life in the area at that time.

It is particularly sad that this copy of June 1915 recorded the death of Lady St Davids eldest son, only a few months after her own death. She and her two sons are commemorated in our church with a plaque, both the boys died in the first World War.

Born in the Eastend of London her parents were Isidor and Fanny Gerstenberg, Jewish immigrants from Poland. Her father was a Merchant Banker in the City and friend and associate of the Baring Brothers, Warburgs, Samuels, etc.[1]

She married John Wynford Philipps, eldest son of Erasmus Philipps Vicar of Warminster. Lord St David remarried within 12months of her death.

NORA ST. DAVIDS.
IN MEMORY. MARCH 30, 1915.

Lydstep Estate was sold by Public Auction in 1927.

Leonora St Davids was the force behind the Welsh Nursing Association and its placement of a qualified nurse in every Welsh Village. This was the subject of the BBC drama series 'District Nurse' starring Nerys Hughes. However, it was 1930 before the Council considered acquiring a District Nurse for Penally.

---

1. Ref: Liz Thompson of the Rideway Society.

There were only a handful of copies printed and few of them remain in existence, again they would have been a useful reference of the early years of the First World War.

OUR VILLAGE SOCIETY CHRONICLE

(MANORBIER, PENALLY, ST. FLORENCE, AND GUMFRESTON).

NO. 9.	JUNE, 1915.	VOL. III.

CONTENTS.

In Memory - - - - - 1	The Duty of the Church in the Present	
Nora St. Davids: In Memory - - 2	Crisis - - - - -	9
A Personal Sketch - - - 3	Notes from Our Villages—	
In Memoriam - - - - 3	Manorbier - - -	10
The Reunion Society - - - 4	Penally - - -	12
Greatness - - - - - 6	St. Florence - - -	12
Capt. Roland Philipps' Letter - 7		
Unto Life - - - - - 7	Our Voluntary Aid Detachment -	13
Lydstep Burrows - - - - 8	Quotation - - - -	13
Notes from the Front - - - 8	Daffodils - - - -	14

IN MEMORY.

Petty Officer DAVID JAMES, killed in action on the "Kennet" on August 22, 1914, aged 37. Grandson of Mrs. James, St. Florence.

WILLIAM SHIPLEY, Royal Navy, aged 28, husband of Mary Davies, Manorbier; went down in H.M.S. "Good Hope" on November 1, 1914.

CHARLES ALLEN, Royal Engineers, aged 44, eldest son of Mr. and Mrs. William Allen, Manorbier; died from wounds December 7, 1914.

WILFRED JOHN, 2nd Welsh Regiment, aged 28, second son of Mr. and Mrs. William John, Manorbier; killed in action in France on May 9, 1915.

Captain the Hon. COLWYN ERASMUS ARNOLD PHILIPPS, Royal Horse Guards, aged 26, elder son of Lord and Lady St. Davids, killed in action near Ypres on Ascension Day, May 13, 1915.

" There is no death : what seems so is transition."

12	OUR VILLAGE SOCIETY CHRONICLE.

George Gwyther
Arthur Roblin
Lance-Corpl. R. Thomas
J. W. Thomas
J. A. Wharton
J. Collins
Jack Brooks
Jack Cocker
William Brown
George Brace
Charles John
John Thomas
Peter Callaghan
Bertie Richards
William John

PENALLY.

THE Church was, as usual, beautifully decorated for Easter. A handsome floral cross adorned the east end. The collections were given to the National School Building Fund.

Our village has become quite noted of late in being able to boast of a lady churchwarden. So far only two places in Pembrokeshire can claim this distinction. Miss Clifton, who holds the position, takes the place of Mr. Hugh Angell, who has obtained a commission in the Royal Field Artillery, and has been in training for some months past. Mr. Angell undertook so many rôles in the village, and performed the duties relating to them so willingly, that his presence is much missed. We all wish him a speedy and safe return.

The weekly social evenings for the benefit of the soldiers have been well attended. Many parishioners and others have helped to make the time pleasant and successful. The soldiers have been most grateful for the kindness shown to them on these occasions.

On Friday, April 24th, one of these "evenings" was arranged for the benefit of a recently made widow with seven children. After expenses had been paid (including light refreshments) the sum of £1 19s. 6d. was realized. This, with a donation of 5s., was handed over, as well as a further gift from the vicar, who made it up to a nice round sum of money. On this occasion the soldiers attended in full force.

We have to record the death of Mrs. Voyle, of "The Cottage," who was for many years a school manager. She was a kind friend to the Church and the poor. For some time ill-health had compelled her to lead a very quiet and retiring life. Much sympathy is felt for the Misses Voyle.

Miss James has resigned her duties as teacher in the school through ill-health. This is much to be regretted, as her work was so thorough and efficient. It is to be hoped that she will soon become strong and well again.

The following communication has been received by Mrs. Osborne from Colonel Trower :—"I am directed to thank you for four pairs socks, four pairs mittens, one scarf made by the school children of Penally."

ROLL OF HONOUR.

Army.

Lieut. Hugh Angell, Royal Field Artillery.
Lieut. V. Hill-Lowe, Royal Irish Horse.
William Cavill, Royal Garrison Artillery (T.F.)
Dennis Donoghue, Royal Garrison Artillery (T.F.)
Robert Davies, Army Service Corps.
Richard Eagle, Welsh Regiment.
Frederick Evans, Welsh Regiment.
William Evans, Welsh Regiment.
Albert Edwards, Royal Engineers.
Percy Gardiner, Royal Engineers.
Thomas Griffiths, Royal Garrison Artillery (T.F.)
William Griffiths, Royal Garrison Artillery (T.F.)
Herbert Griffiths, Pembrokeshire Yeomanry.
Thomas Hackett, Grenadier Guards.
John Harries, Royal Garrison Artillery.
Frederick Gay, City of London.
Arthur James, Army Service Corps.
John John, Army Service Corps.
Arthur Morgan, Army Service Corps.
Reginald Morris, Army Service Corps.
William Phillips, Army Service Corps.
George Rees, Pembrokeshire Yeomanry.
Charles Taylor, Welsh Fusiliers.
William Torrington, Welsh Regiment.
James Wickland, Army Service Corps.
George Williams, Pembrokeshire Yeomanry.

Navy.

William Donoghue, H.M.S. Leopard.
Arthur Harries, changed ship, name unknown.
Alfred Phillips, H.M.S. Prince George.
George Thompson, H.M.S. Laconia.
John Williams, training ship.

ST. FLORENCE.

DEATH OF LADY ST. DAVIDS—Quite a gloom was cast over this parish when the sad news of the death of Lady St. Davids became generally known. Ever aiming to raise the ideals of the inhabitants of these parishes, and to assist in every good cause for the welfare of the community, her memory will long be cherished. It is some consolation, however, to know that the

The following account of the three-day celebration of Colwyn Philipps' 21st birthday took place in May 1911. Impossible to read without a magnifying glass, but the contents give an idea of the scale of the three day party.

Edwardian Penally (from 1901)

LORD ST. DAVIDS' HEIR

COMING OF AGE CELEBRATION:

Second Day's Proceeding:

CONCERT AND BALL.

The Romance of Lydstep

(BY OUR SPECIAL CORRESPONDENT.)

LYDSTEP, Monday Evening. To-day the weather has shown considerable improvement over that which was experienced on Saturday, so that the large house party which is staying at Lydstep Haven for the celebrations in connection with the coming of age of the eldest son of Lord and Lady St. Davids have been able to see something of the magnificent coast scenery. The only drawback to outdoor exercise to-day has been a bitterly old wind, which, since last night, has been roaring around the cliff top. This afternoon the Hon. Colwyn Philipps slipped away from its guests for a short time for the purpose of putting in an appearance at the Pembroke at stock show, where farmers from all over the county have assembled. This thoughtful act on the part of Mr Philipps is quite characteristic of him.

This evening Lydstep Haven is the scene of largely attended concert and ball, and from 7 to 9 o'clock the guests arrived in motors and takes from all parts of the county.

With regard to the house party, whose ames were published yesterday, I should add that the Dowager Lady Wynford was at the last moment unavoidably prevented from coming, and telegraphed her regrets. Col. Ivor hilipps, D.S.O., M.P., and Mrs Philipps and liss Philipps are entertaining relatives with 'iends, including Mr and Mrs Delme Dawes-vans, Mr John Godsal, Miss Grace Godsal, nd Mr Patrick Mundy at Cosheston Hall.

The guests present at the ball this evening re as follow :—Lady Scourfield, Mrs Lewis, lean Castle ; Mr Seymour Allen, of Cres-lly, M.F.H., Mr Hugh Allen, Mr and Mrs lasey, Cuffern, Mr and Mrs Summers, he Hon. Colwyn Philipps, the Hon. Roland hilipps, Sir James and the Hon. Lady hilipps, Colonel Ivor Philipps, D.S.O., M.P., rs and Miss Philipps, General and Mrs urteis, Colonel, Mrs. and Miss Mire-use, Colonel and Mrs Lawrie, Colonel d Mrs Taylor, Colonel and Mrs rower, Colonel and Mrs Frank Allen, olonel and Mrs Harries, Colonel and Mrs oyle, Colonel, Mrs. and Miss Denn, Colonel loyd Lindsay, Major Simpson D.S.O. (Mayor 'Bath), and Miss Marshall, Major Cass, ajor Glascot, Major and Mrs Corbett, aptain and Mrs Henderson, Captain and Mrs ent, Captain and Mrs Jordan, Captain and rs Mundy and Mr P. Mundy, Captain and rs Hunter, Captain Veal, Captain Forster, aptain Mathias, the Rector of Tenby, Mr N. betwode Ram, Mr and Miss Gilbert Harries, Mr miningham, Mr, Mrs and Miss Bowen Sem-ers, Mrs W. F. Roch of Bridell, Mr Lewis owen, Mr, Mrs and Miss Gilbert Harries, Mr d Mrs Harries, Mr, Mrs and the Misses Har-ty, Mr and Mrs Delme-Davies-Evans, Mrs 'right, Mr and Miss Smallpiece, Mrs Bur-tt, Mr and Mrs Godsal, Mr Barrett, Mr rthur Pelly, Mr Gerald Grove, Mr Charles secelles, Mr C. Lewis (Stradey Castle), Mr urroughs, Lieut. Vaughan, the Rev. D. orris and Miss Clifton, the Rev. and Mrs eaver, the Rev. G. Rowe and Mrs Rowe, r and Mrs Austin, Mr and Mrs Fred imners, Mrs Mathias, Dr. and Mrs Mathias, e Misses Mathias, Mrs and Miss Rayner 'ood, Mrs Stokes, Mr and Mrs Mathias homas, Mr L. Mathias Thomas, Mr and Mrs ugh Thomas, Mr Loftus Adams, Miss Allen, iss Choate, Mr W. Eaton Evans, Mr and Mrs

Roch, Mr and Mrs Yorke, Mr H. M. Harries, Mr Kelly, Mr C Barclay, Mr Clement Williams, Mr and Mrs David Harrison, Dr. and Mrs Hamilton, Dr., Mrs. and Miss Knowling, Mr and Mrs Bryant, Dr. and Mrs and Miss Saunders, Mrs and Miss Jones, Miss Milward, Dr. and Mrs Williams.

THE CONCERT.

At 9 o'clock a concert was held, at which the programme was as follows :—
1.—" The Lord High Executioner " ....Sullivan
 Welsh Glee Singers.
2—(a) " Suo-gan " ....Old Welsh Folk Songs
 (b) " Y Gwcw Fach " ....Old Welsh Folk Songs
 Miss Dilys Jones.
3—" In Absence " ....Buck
 Welsh Glee Singers.
4—(a) " Lungi dal caro bene " ....A. L.
 (b) " I'll rock you to rest " ....Stanford
 (c) " When Childer Plays " ....Watford Davies
 Miss Dilys Jones.
5—(a) " Ar Hyd y Nos." (b) " Men of Harlech," Evans
 Welsh Glee Singers.
6—(a) " Bugail yr Hafod " ....Old Welsh Folk Songs
 (b) " Yr Hufen Melyn " ....
 Miss Dilys Jones.
7—(a) " Stars of the Summer Night " ....Hatton
 Welsh Glee Singers.
 " Land of my Fathers."

The concert was held in the library and billiard-room, which were thrown into one, and which provided ample accommodation, and formed the prettiest apartment imaginable. The concert, for which a small platform had been erected in the window, lasted about an hour and a half, and the artistes were very heartily applauded.

THE BALL.

Dancing began at 10.30 in the library of the splendid orchestra of Mr Fred Roberts, of Cardiff, who, with his instrumentalists, was ensconced in the large music gallery in the library. The excellent programme of dance music which they provided was as follows :— 1, valse, " La Faste des Roses " ; 2, valse, " Chanson de mon Cœur " ; 3, two-step, " Hobomoko " ; 4, valse, " Verschmähte Liebe " ; 5, lancers, " Our Miss Gibbs " ; 6, valse, " Du me Disait " ; 7, valse, " The Drunk' Prayer "; 8, two-step, " Yip-i-addy-i-ay "; 9, valse, " Phryne "; 10, valse, " Lisiletta "; 11, valse, " Gold and Silver "; 12, valse, " Vision of Salome"; 13, two-step, " I'm afraid to come home in the dark "; 14, valse, " The Dollar Princess "; 15, lancers, " Havana "; 16, valse, " Mandalay "; 17, two-step, " Teddy Bear's Picnic "; 18, valse, " Longe D'Antoine "; 19, valse, " Venus on Earth "; 20, valse, " Tales of Hoffmann."

The scene when the dancing was in progress was animated and beautiful in the extreme. The library and billiard room had been most tastefully decorated by Mr Jensen, the head gardener. The general scheme of decoration was of yellow chrysanthemums and ferns, with flemish hyacinths, etc.

From their massive gilt frames on the walls above the ancestors of the Philipps family looked down in state on the merry scenes. Perhaps a word or so may be said at this point regarding a few of Lord St. Davids' very fine pictures. One of the most notable in the library is an oil painting of the famous Pembrokeshire historian, Richard Fenton, by Sir William Beechey, who was the Court painter to King George IV. On either side are two of Lord St. Davids' ancestors. One of them, Lord Chief Justice Best, who was afterwards created Lord Wynford, was his Lordship's great-grand-father, and the other is of Sir William Chappell, a former judge of the King's Bench. In another part of the room is a fine portrait of that fine old warrior General Richard Philipps, who distinguished himself under William of Orange, and who raised the 40th Regiment. On another part of the same wall is an excellent painting of Colonel Ivor Philipps in Yeomanry uniform. On the staircase there are some more very interesting family pictures, including one of the Vicomte de Fonblanque, a Huguenot ancestor of Lord St. Davids'. There is a beautiful painting of Lord St. Davids himself, which was presented to him some time ago by a number of friends in London. At the top of the staircase are paintings of the Rev. Sir James Erasmus Philipps and the Hon. Lady Philipps, whilst another notable piece of work is a very fine painting of Lady St. Davids by Edwin Long, R.A. There are many other beautiful pictures at Lydstep Haven, but space does not permit of mention in the present occasion of more than one or two in the drawing room, at the end of which the place of honour is accorded to the " Blue Angel," a magnificent and characteristic example of the work of the late Sir E. Burne-Jones, R.A., and a very charming portrait by Mrs Swinerton of the Hon. Colwyn Philipps when a boy.

At the ball, as at the concert, everything passed off in the most enjoyable manner. On Tuesday's celebrations will be on a very large scale, for there will be luncheon to several hundred guests at one o'clock, later a concert and reception to members of the village societies of Manorbier, Penally, and St. Florence. Prior to the luncheon, a presentation will be made to Mr Colwyn Philipps by the tradesmen of Tenby.

Imagine such a three-day event today!

Viscount St Davids' second wife was Lady Elizabeth Rawden Hastings, Baroness Strange of Knockyn and Hungerford. She was the first Peeress to speak in the House of Lords and that speech (which was much praised) was written for her by our own local historian, Dillwyn Miles.

There was a County request in 1916 for 'a house to house enquiry as to what women were prepared to work on farms for the War effort?' The parish council replied that 'there were no women as would undertake the work.'

As early as 1914 the parish had wanted to build some 15 cottages, as, and when, required, nothing was done however because of the war. In 1919, two sites were considered suitable, Glanymor Gardens, belonging to Captain Angell, and part of a field, belonging to the Picton Estate, and the parish asked the Rural District Council what was being done about a housing scheme for the village? They replied, asking how many were required, and the parish asked for '20 working class', but many years passed before anything happened.

However, Mortimer Allen, the photographer of Tenby, had built some new 'bungalows' in Court Farm orchard and in 1922 he asked for a water supply to them. Council agreed, with permission of Mr Phillips of Court Farm, to extend the pipe from his house at 10 shillings a year to the bungalows. Was this an early development with tourists in mind?

They were round houses with corrugated iron roofs, there were three of them, and they were referred to as 'the nest' by the locals. They must be one of the best-kept secrets in the village because few people today remember them, and unfortunately, there do not seem to be any photographs either.

Meanwhile, the school had also modernised, from obtaining a washing bowl and a water can in 1900 to a visit from the Medical Officer once a year as well as a visit from the District Nurse, which ensured isolation when a disease broke out.

Sadly, the winter months continued to make children very ill indeed with whooping cough and scarlet fever, and diphtheria claiming a few lives, but the summer months brought endless joys.

The one big distraction that no one could ignore was when the cavalry were camping in nearby 'yeomanry' field, which could be seen and heard from the school. So school closed early, and the children were permitted to watch their activities. This continued throughout May and June. Sometimes there were so many horses on the road it was unsafe for the children and the school had to close altogether.

These were the pupils in Mrs Osborne's last year of 1929. Notice the shining boots. (From Gwladys Evans collection).

Back Row: Amy Edwards. ? ? ? Margery Morris ? ? ?
Middle: Mary Rees. Gwen Haines. ? Hugh Williams. Claude Griffiths. Fred Williams. Bill Haines. Ann Morton. Doris Edwards. Betty Phillips. Molly Harris. Maisie Morgan.
Front: Eileen Ollen. Gwladys James. Betty Davies. ? Barbara Phillips. Molly Harris. ? ? John Morton. ? ? ? Leslie Edwards.

A school syllabus was drawn up, subjects were: English. Arithmetic, Geography, Observation, Singing, Brush drawing, Needlework and PT (breathing).

By 1912 holidays stretched to 5 weeks.

At the end of the War, in 1919, Allotments for food production were to occupy the council meetings over the years, and they thrived right up until the Second World War, by which time, there were so few men to work them, they fell into disuse.

Tourists must have been around in some numbers at that early date, a chip potato van had stood at the Crown Inn in the summer of 1922 and Captain Angell proposed the clerk should write to the owner of the land, Mr Hall, requesting that he should not allow this in the future! It was at this time that Hermann Thomas declared the village pump had worn out and he could do no more.

Mortimer Allen had died in 1927, and Mr Brace, who was then at Court Farm, would not pay the water charge, so houses at 'the nest' were cut off. Neither would he consent to carts going through the gateway to the footpath and the allotments, and suggested that a properly fenced alternative should be provided.

There had always been controversy about the public use of the path to the beach through Court Farm, and when motorcars started to use it too, Sackville Owen on behalf of Picton Estate, protested that the practice must stop! The parish council however claimed 'existing users' rights.

Colonel John Groves at Lydstep Haven also complained about the public use of his road to the beach, but he was content with a notice that all dogs must be under control.

Parish Council members in the twenties were Captain Angell, J. W. Brown, T. Morgan, T. Edwards, G. Griffiths, E. P. Gardner, A. E. Protheroe, D. Griffiths, and Mr Shanklin. Meetings were still being held in the schoolroom.

About 1923 they got around to discussing ways and means of getting a dead body conveyed for burial. A hand bier had been thought appropriate, but there were few subscriptions towards it, only £3 from Edward St Davids, £1 from Lloyd George and £1 from Sackville Owen (Picton Estate).

Until that time, Mrs Edwards of Rock Villa was called to tend the dying, which would mean, apart from nursing and caring for them in their last hours, she would 'lay them out', for viewing in the family home, until the day of the funeral. Then, bearers carried the coffin on their shoulders, from the house to the Church, if it was not too great a distance.

This practice continued until motorcars solved the dilemma, but they

Edwardian Penally (from 1901)

Back Row: Tom Williams. Jessie Broad. Percy Gardener. Herbert Griffiths. Mr Hayes. Mr Barson. Mr Rixon. Mr Watts. Mr Odd. Middle Row: George Griffiths. Bill Phillips. Eric Haines. Bill Griffiths. Mr Butler. Charlie Phillips. Tom Phillips. Mr Edwards. Tom Morton. Ivor Morris. Arthur James. Mr Allen. Front Row: Rev. Jones. Billy Butland. Mr Morgan. Mr Edwards. Albert Edwards. Tom Lewis. Fred Morgan. Mr Phillips. Mr Bowen. Mr Hinds. Mr Phillips. Mr Allen. Capt. Angell. (Picture from Guladys Evans' collection).

131

caused a great dust, and now there was a need for tarmacadam. The council wrote to the Automobile Club calling their attention to the state of their signposts in the village in 1927.

The vexed question of a water supply and its costs went back and fore between the R.D.C. and the parish. The habit had been for the parish to pay for pipes and the laying of them, but volunteers were to dig and cover them.

They received an irate letter from Mr Flynn of Kenystyle, slamming 'private keyholders to the supply, namely three parish councillors, their relatives and friends. "Ordinary people like himself, have to walk half a mile and carry water, when it runs past his house!"

Even though the parish council could not afford to spend, as they would have wished, on improving the water situation, they were very glad of any help they could wangle from the R.D.C. who very reasonably felt they were looking after the village.

In 1923 the parish had sent a letter to the R.D.C. wishing to know on what authority they claimed ownership of the water supply at the village pump, when the pump and supply was put up by voluntary contribution and therefore the parish claimed both as their own property.

Finally, there was a Government grant of 33¼% towards water schemes, and it seemed an end to the matter locally, but in 1927 there was a proposal to lay water from Frankleston to Holloway by the County Council for £40, and still it was required that volunteers attend to backfill, etc.

This seems to be the right place in the story to expand on some of the characters, still remembered, who lived in the parish in the first half of the 20th century.

Hugh William Cumming Angell, d.1941.

A very large, florid man. He and his wife, Edith lived first at 1 and then 7 Giltar Terrace, and kept a servant, who lived at Picton Cottage with the Haines family. (He is seen in two of the pictures illustrated.) He also kept monkeys.

He was an early parish councilor, church councilor, trustee of the Cooke Estate, and editor and secretary of the *Parish Chronicle*, until he obtained a commission in the Royal Field Artillery before 1915. He survived the Great War, but it may be that he suffered delayed shock, which showed in later years.

There were 3 people in the village with cars, Sir David Hughes Morgan at the Manor, Major Saurin at the Abbey and Captain Angell on the Terrace. No driving tests or drink-drive laws in those days. Captain Angell was car crazy. A great friend of Graham Ace of Tenby, he had a little chalet closed to Ace's Garage where he would stay if he felt unable to drive back to Penally.

Towards the end of his life, when he lived at Four Winds, he suffered a lot and was terrified to be left alone. He employed men from the village, two at a time, to spend the hours of darkness with him. He liked to sit up in bed while they pushed the bed around the room and he clutched an imaginary steering wheel. He had done so much for the village all his life, when he died in 1941, I am sure his passing was sorely felt.

He is buried at the parish church.

Doctor David Charles Mathias, born in 1878 in Llanstadwell.
He was the son of Charles Mathias, Surgeon Major (Indian Army) born at Paradise House in Gloucester, the owner of Holloway, Frankleston and the Marshlands, and Marianne his wife. Both parents are buried in Penally, although their mother, Marianne, died many years later.

Dr Charlie was the eldest of four boys. His youngest brother Hugh, was to become a renowned Surgeon. They were both six foot three inches tall, but otherwise chalk and cheese in temperament. Both served in the 1914-18 World War in the RAMC.

The middle two sons were born at Waterwynch where the family lived for ten years or so, and then they moved to Fern House in the village where Hugh was born in 1888, the year his father died. Hugh was expected to practice in London, but chose to join Charles in his Tenby based surgery, so local people had the benefit of his expertise in the local Cottage Hospital. Charles preferred to work as a family doctor and enjoyed making house-calls.

Always known as Dr Charlie, he made his calls with his two spaniels in tow. A gruff man, who could be very rude, but was devoted to his patients. He drove a blue car, registration DE 67 and never drank any water other than from the village pump opposite the Crown Inn. As well as all the marshland and Holloway he had the land where Strawberry Gardens is now built and grew all his food up there and kept horses. One could say that he was an early conservationist![2]

I found these headlines in the *Tenby Observer* of October 1912:

**A Tenby Sensation
Well known Doctor Shot**

It seems he was shot on the threshold of his house in St Julian St, he was severely wounded above the knee with a soft nose bullet.

His assailant was Thomas Llewellyn from Marsh Road who succeeded in getting away. He was captured within the hour and locked up.

Poor old Llewellyn was weak minded but accused of attempted murder and after a trial was detained during his Majesties pleasure to receive proper care. The doctor took some time to recover fully.

There are many stories about his forthright turn of phrase, for example at Holloway Farm, there was a gateway into one of the fields which needed painting. It was alongside the first house in school lane, recently built, and occupied by a man he disliked, known locally as 'pop' Howells who owned the Softdrink Works in Tenby, but more respectfully, Councillor H. Howells. When he asked the doctor what colour he intended to paint the gate, Doctor Charlie said rudely 'monkey's-arse blue.'

Ernie Griffiths – from Malvern Lodge (the grandfather of actor Kenneth Griffith) was a stone-mason. He was working on the

---
2. Notes from Ruth Griffiths.

roof of Mrs Ramsdens house (now Mrs Whitehead's) when Dr Charlie was walking up School Lane. Dr Charlie shouted "None of your shoddy work now Griffiths, do you hear what I say?" Ernie replied: "My shoddy work is up here for everyone to see, your shoddy work is 6ft under."

A family called Brace lived up on the Ridgeway, and when the father died he left a frail widow and three teenage boys with no income. Dr Charlie told the boys to report to the Golf Club where he was secretary at the time, and work was found for them as groundsmen. They were paid, but whether by the Club, or the doctor, is not known.

He certainly was not all bad, in fact he was much loved and his 'doctoring' was highly regarded. There are many testimonies to his kindness.

He was also a fine golfer and played for Cambridge University as a young man. He was secretary of Tenby Golf Club for over 26 years and was described in an article in *Golf World* (1973) as 'the last great dictator'. He regarded the golf club as his own private property, he even grazed his sheep on the course. He cared nothing for the clubhouse or the social side of things and most of the fierce hazards on the course were his creations. The bunkers on the right of the 18th green are known as 'Charlies Whiskers'. When he left the Club in some acrimony, he took holes 15, 16, and 17, with him, these holes lay in what today we know as Kiln Park Caravan Site, which may never have existed had he not done so. However, to many of the older members, he had made Tenby Golf Club the best in Wales, maybe even in Britain.

Dr Charlie had a severe car accident in 1944, and although he then retired, he continued serving the locality as a rebel Councillor.

His passing made the front page in the *Tenby Observer*: "No ordinary man, tough, fearless and with little respect for authority. When he agreed to stand for the Council, he issued no election notice, solicited no votes, asked no favours and was top of the poll. He thrived on controversy."

He died in 1954, and was cremated in Pontypridd leaving a brother and two daughters, Cynthia and Joyce. His brother Hugh FRCS, had a quiet voice and smoked a pipe. He had a handicap of 2, unlike Charlie who was never known to take a handicap. Hugh died in 1963.

The Mathias Estate covered most of the area North of the village, from Frankleston right round to the end of the golf course, taking in 1 & 2

Frankleston Cottages, Frankleston House, Red House, Ridgeway End, Rosewood Cottage, Holloway Farm, Fern House, Court Farm and cliffland, The W.I. Hall, Blackrock Quarry, and all the marshland.

The family had owned most of the land since 1822, and no doubt benefited from the interest of the Army, Railway, Quarries and Caravans over the years.

Ethel Georgina De N. Clifton was the stepdaughter of David Melville Morris, Vicar of St Nicholas from 1873-1923. After the vicar was widowed, she was his constant companion at all social functions

A striking character, she wore a bright ginger wig and smoked De-Reske Minor's incessantly. She played the organ at church over a period of 50 years and this is commemorated with a blower for the organ and an inscription. She also took an interest in the school and played an active role in village life. She lived at 'Llyswen' and was very strict on 'good manners'. When she died in 1949 she left a charity to the poor of the village at Christmas time.

Heather Angel was a film star who was the niece of the Angel family living at Glanymor in the 1930's. She quite often used to visit them, and Irene Wall who ran the Crown Inn, remembers her coming into the bar. She died in California in 1987. Considered a great beauty, she was superceded by Madeleine Carroll. She starred in 'Berkeley Square', 'The Informer', and 'The Mystery of Edwin Drood' and later in her career, she became familiar to television audiences as the housekeeper in the long running 'Peyton Place'.

She also featured in the first film called 'The last of the Mohicans' and my colleague Ruth Griffiths has a video tape of it.

* * *

A nonsense poem written about this time, from the local newspaper:

There was a young man from Penally,
Who with two young ladies was pally
One was called Sally who lived in the Alley,
And Lily lived down in the valley

It worried the chap from Penally
That Lily should live in the valley
He said 'It is silly to go out with Lily
When I live much nearer to Sally.'

Then one day this youth from Penally
Took a trip. To the house in the valley,
And there he found Lily, with a fellow named Billy,
So he hurried straight back to the alley.

He asked all the neighbours for Sally
They said 'She has gone from the alley;
A fellow named Willy, a cousin of Billy,
Took Sally away to the valley.'

The distracted young man from Penally
Spent his time twixt the alley and valley,
But he never saw Willie or Lily orBilly
Or even the light-hearted Sally.

So he went right away from Penally
From the valley, the alley and Sally
Hung himself from a post.
And gave up the ghost,
And the trumpeters sounded reveille.

'WOOLHOUSE'

William Heurtly Marmaduke Roberts, 1868-1951

The following very sad account of the demise of the local 'basket weaver' appeared in the *Tenby Observer* on January 5th 1951.

Man who might have been Mayor died a recluse

Heurtly Roberts is dead. His end came in a manner which many of his friends and contemporaries feared it would. He was found in bed in the isolated cottage where he lived alone. He had been dead about five days.

William Heurtly Marmaduke Roberts was known to younger generations of Tenby folk as something of an incongruous figure. He was an old man although he did not look his 83 years.

He was dishevelled, bearded and unkempt, yet his voice was polished and cultured, belied only by his impressive sounding name.

He was born in St. Florence. As a young man he went to London. There he worked in a bank. He found that the work did not suit his health and he returned to Tenby to follow the rural craft of basket making, working with his father in St. Florence.

SKILLED CRAFTSMAN

He became a very skilled craftsman and at one time had a contract for making baskets for the Imperial Hotel.

After his marriage he lived in Park Place.

It was in 1920 that he was first elected to the Tenby Town Council. In all, he fought five elections, the last in 1933, and on each occasion he was successful.

But despite his series of successes, he always left the polling booths after voting had finished, never remaining to witness the count or hear the poll declared.

He was not the most garrulous of councillors. For those who know the council chamber, he sat at the end of the table nearest the fire. During discussions he would frequently leave the table completely, draw his chair up to the fire and sit there pensively smoking his pipe and listening to the deliberations of his colleagues. When they had finished, he would add his observations in rather ponderous tones and language.

Perhaps his effort on the Council which brought him most fame was that which resulted in the extension of the Walk from the Esplanade down to the South Beach, thus avoiding elderly folk and women with children having to make their final descent to the beach by means of a flight of steep steps.

ROBERT'S WALK

In recognition of his idea, townspeople gratefully christened the additional part of the slipway "Roberts' Walk."

Although he was at one time one of the senior members of the Council he was never elected Mayor.

After the death of his wife, he became less careful about his appearance and eventually he left Tenby to live in a tiny two-roomed cottage in the St. Florence area. It was called The Quay and lay in a secluded spot off the Hoyle's Mouth Lane, mid-way between Holloway and St. Florence.

He frequently walked into Tenby to do his shopping, however.

It was when his sister, Mrs. Shears, who lives in St. Florence, received no news of him for several days that she became alarmed. She rang Trefloyne Farm, the residence of Dr. Thomas, who owns the cottage. A workman was sent over to look for Mr. Roberts on Saturday morning. Accompanied by a couple of companions, he went into the cottage and discovered that Mr. Roberts was dead.

The police were informed and Police Sergeant W. A. Thomas and Dr. M. O. Evans went out to the cottage from Tenby.

MONEY FOUND

They found Mr. Roberts clad only in a shirt, lying on the bed under two ragged blankets. The room was in a very neglected condition. There was little food in the house and the only fuel was wood.

Yet under the mattress they discovered a Post Office Savings Bank book with a credit balance of £155 and also a £5 note, 19 £ notes and eight 10/- notes (a total of £28).

The second room of the cottage Mr. Roberts used as a workshop, for he continued his basket making until the end. One cot-like basket remained there half-finished.

The body was later conveyed to the Tenby mortuary where it remained until the funeral on Wednesday afternoon.

For many years to come the name of Heurtly Roberts will be recalled when talk turns to characters of the Tenby Council Chamber. And those who remember him will shake their heads in regret that a man who might have made so much of life should have ended his days in such distressing circumstances.

THE FUNERAL

Only one member of the Town Council attended the funeral, which took place on Wednesday afternoon at Tenby cemetery. He was Alderman T. George Thomas, who was a member of the Council in Mr. Roberts' time.

Others present were relatives and Mr. Jack Beynon, of St. John's Hill, Tenby.

The Rector of Tenby (Rev. H. J. B. Hallam, M.A.), officiated.

The Town Council paid tribute to Mr. Roberts at their meeting on Tuesday, when the Mayor referred to the passing of one of their old and respected members. A vote of condolence was passed with all present standing in silent tribute.

Vernon Evans of Bubbleton, Laurie's son, recalls frequently seeing Heurtly Roberts waiting for the afternoon train to pass through a field of his at Bubbleton, from which someone would throw a bundle which Heurtly picked up. He was the last resident of Quay Cottage.

Penally water diviner claims oil discovery

'Response' so strong, it strained his side!

A 76-year-old Penally man, Mr. Joseph Phillips, of The Commons, has struck oil! He claims that it runs down in three courses from Penhoyle, near St. Forence, to spots on the Penally coast where it enters the sea.

A small piece "V" shaped twig was the only aid silver-haired, moustached Mr. Phillips had in making his remarkable discovery. For although he has been a water diviner for over twenty years, he had not until a few years ago known that he was also able to detect other substances as well.

The oil was one of them. But he told an "Observer" reporter this week that his twig will respond to any mineral or ore which is in the ground, regardless of whether it is solid or fluid.

He has been able to pin-point the position at which the land contains iron, copper, silver—and even gold—will cause his twig to bend upwards in a fascinating manner. "But," he remarked drily, "I haven't been really able to test it on gold yet."

How does he differentiate between the different materials which his twig indicates? Astute Mr. Phillips keeps it a secret, but he revealed to our reporter that it lies in the number of times the twig will bend upwards.

Oil is far more powerful than water, he says, and added that if a water-main ran over a course of oil the stick would react to the oil—although it lay underneath.

"To tell you how strong it is " went on the sturdily built ex-railway head ganger, " when I decided to track down the full extent of this oil course I found the whole of my left side being effected by the strain. My eye went weak and in the end I had to give it up. In fact I haven't tried it on oil since."

LATE DISCOVERY

Strangely, Mr. Phillips did not discover his amazing gift until he was in his middle fifties. And it was not until much later that he found that he seemed to have developed his power into locating other substances as well.

He says that it is immaterial what kind of stick one uses—blackthorn, willow, or privet are all alike to him.

"But," he warned, " don't take too thick a stick, otherwise it will bend your fingers off. Once the stick finds something, nothing will stop it bending yours, and if you curl your fingers round it like I do your fingers will go as well!"

Mr. Phillips has utilised his gift over the years by assisting farmers to find water and by selecting the most profitable spots for a Tenby contracting firm to sink wells. But when he first got an inkling that there was something different from water in the fields and cliffs stretching away in front of his house, he was puzzled for a while.

Then he noticed that his rod twisted in a similar manner when he held it near petrol. He tested the fields again, and then it struck him—he had struck oil. Examination of surface water on the fields assured him that he had not been mistaken, for they contained a distinct trace of the substance.

Although he is unable to say how rich the seams are, he has estimated roughly that they lie about 150 feet deep and are in the nature of a narrow river.

Our reporter tried to divine a well of deep water at the foot of Mr. Phillips' garden—but the rod remained straight and rigid. Didn't even twitch!

Water-Diviner Joseph Phillips, b.1876. He lived at 2 Bower Cottages with his wife Ellen. This was reported about 1952 in the local paper.

We can boast another 'Diviner' in the village in Sidney Thomas who discovered water on Caldey Island in the 1970's, thereby saving the monks a great deal of money, but that story is beyond our brief.

Chapter 6

George VI to Elizabeth II (1930-53)

A NATURAL DIVISION in the story of the village comes about after the years of the 'great depression' at the end of the 1920's. Perhaps it was through the cinema that peoples expectations were higher than ever before, but a need to become modern was the most important thing in most minds. The village had hardly altered, but at this time some new houses were appearing.

The Allen family had a group of bungalows built about 1920 called Kenystyle, possibly after the Kenyan colonial style? They had water tanks on their flat rooves. Kenneth Griffiths, the actor and director of films, lived in one of them as a child. He recalls in his book *The Fool's Pardon*, that Major Julian Allen was something of an inventor, having built his own Catamaran, as well as a sand yacht which they raced to great effect on the South Beach. I believe the Allen's also built the trio of houses known as Causway cottages.

'Bron-Llwyn', where Molly Whitehead lives, was built in 1921 for the Ramsden family. It was designed by the architect Glover Thomas, as was 'The Retreat' which was built the same year and where he chose to live himself. Ida Jones, the artist, had 'Brackenlea' built in 1925.

Sidney Watts, Penally's own coal merchant from 1923 to 1940, was also a builder. He left his mark in such bungalows as 'Caldey View' and 'Avebury' with its charming veranda. I am told these houses were erected on Dr Mathias's land, and the freehold and 'rights of way' were withheld.

'Four Winds' a very different house, was romantically built on the edge of Black Rock by Loftus Adams of Holyland, for his daughter on her impending marriage. This was in 1929. The young couple spent three months at 'The Mount' whilst the house was being finished, and a further three months living in it, only to become divorced. A highly gossipy matter in those days.

Hugh Angell lived there in the late thirties, and ended his days there. Today, the Hilling family own Four Winds, the same name family that lived in Penally in the 17th century.

E. J. Head RA, who came to Tenby from Scarborough in the 1880's and taught Augustus John and his sister Gwen, designed the house called 'Wayside'. He died there in 1937 after watching through his window the searchlight excercises by the Territorials in Penally. He is buried in Tenby. He also designed the 'bas-relief' plaque of John Morgan Griffiths which is on the inside wall of the Chapel.

Septimus Clayton lived at Fern House, which still belonged to the Mathias family, and he started a garage on the land adjacent, which by the 1930's was much needed. Tennis courts used to grace that land.

First, Harry Elwood and then Henry Turner followed him, and finally Saunders became the last proprietor. He added 4 more petrol pumps and no doubt would have continued a service for many more years save for the building of the by-pass in the 1960's which took traffic from the village.

The country was experiencing some affluence at this time and the South Wales Electricity Board was a very big employer locally. It took many years to drag every property into the 20th century with this facility, some of us did not enjoy the benefits until the mid-sixties.

In 1930 Tenby Town Council applied for a Crown regulating lease in respect of the foreshore, from the Burrows to Giltar Point. This was to de with extending the borough under section 46 of the Local Government Act of 1929, and Tenby had wasted no time.

Penally Parish Council strongly objected to it being granted, in fact there was a threat that the extension proposed to include all of Penally.

G. Griffiths and Shanklin went to the meeting as parish representatives, but no decision was taken that day. The next year, Captain Angel attended a second meeting at which the proposal was again refused, but the threat remained, and in 1932, delegates were appointed to go to a meeting in Haverfordwest. They were Captain Angell, Sir D. H. Morgan, Major Saurin and Dr D. C. Mathias.

The Reverend J. Williams said: 'we must not lose the best place that the village is noted for, for a quiet holiday'.

In the event, Saurin and Morgan could not attend, and Dr Mathias felt disqualified since he represented the Tenby Golf Club, in fact all three were officers at the Golf Club, so it was left to Hugh Angel alone.

The sands were taken over by Tenby Town Council on April 1st 1934.

The class of 1933.

Back row: Nora Williams. Colwyn Phillips. Wyn Phillips. Ken Edwards. Leslie Edwards. Peter Phillips. Jim Morton. Leslie Edwards (Rock Villa) Leslie Rixon.
Second row: Ted Morton. Thomas Hughes. Barbara Phillips. Joan Phillips. Gwldys James. Marjery Harris. Betty Davies. John Morton. Stanley Edwards. Tom Morton. Fred Evans. Douglas ?
Third row: Jean Hayes. Beryl Luly. Jean Morris. Emeralda Hughes. Enid Edwards. Angela Griffiths. Maisie Edwards. John Watts. Lionel Luly.
Fourth row: Trevor Rixon. Hayden Rdwards. Rosie Evans. Molly Harris. Pat Phillips. Frank Brown. John Hinds. Tommy Morgan.

Some of these children pictured, are also in the earlier photograph of 1929, and it is interesting to see the difference a span of 4 years makes in a child. It is from these children that a great deal of information has been gleaned. Next are the voluntary work-party to clean up around the church sometime in the 1930's, from Gwladys Evans' collection.

Back row, left: Arthur Edwards (Rosewood); Jim Voyle Morris (Court Cottage); Syrme (Alma Cottage); George Haines (Picton House); Brace (Court Farm); Colwyn Morris (Elm House); Arthur James (Penally Stores); Tom Jones (Station House); A. Edwards (Giltar Terr.); Capt. Angel; Rev. S. Jones.
Front row: Stanley Davies (Giltar Cottage); Chas Edwards (Rosewood); Ellis Skyrme (Alma Cottage); Leslie Edwards (Hill Crest); Ivor Morris (Elm House); Tom Phillips (Starvation).

Just prior to this in 1930, an unemployed miner and bare-knuckle fighter from Stepaside, called Attwell, had made an application to hire out ponies on the foreshore, and he also wanted a stall to sell wooden toys.

Attwell was living at West Holloway at this time. This was granted but the following year the parish received another application fom Scourfield of Clover Hill, Carew. The council said 'no' to Scourfield and 'yes' to Attwell. However, the Board of Trade over-rode the decision because they saw it as a monopoly, and they suggested the parish should apply for a Crown regulating lease of the foreshore. It was the same year that Tenby was planing to absorb Penally.

In 1932, Attwell had 6 ponies and 50 deckchairs, but in 1934 he overstepped the parish indulgence and erected a barbed wire fence from the cliffs to the beach road, and was promptly directed by registered letter to clear all obstructions within seven days.

In 1931 there were 2,700 troops, that is to say, 5 Battalions, using the camp. Imagine the effect of all those men on the village. There was work for many laundresses, and during this time the quarries at Kiln Park, which were run by W. H. Phillips & Son were still employing over a hundred men.

A curious snippet from the council records for this period states, that there was to be a National Rat Week for which all poisons would be supplied by the Government, it makes one wonder?

And so time passed with the villagers enjoying the seasons as they had always done, but now, as well as the annual fairs and festivals, were added whist drives, village dances, race meetings, variety concerts, and best of all, the cinema in Tenby. There was also an advance of popular knowledge with well-attended public lectures and travelling libraries.

About 1937 Halliday & England, merchants from Peterborough, arrived at Whitewell Farm. They were the pioneers of growing 'early potatoes'.

This new crop was to have an enormous impact on the farming economy in the County, and literally put Pembrokeshire 'on the map'.

Demonstrations were held at Whitewell for the local farmers, and the new crop eventually gave employment to hundreds of casual workers twice in one season with planting and harvesting.

Robert Halliday and his wife lived at Whitewell. Their neighbour at Bubbleton was Louis Thomas who had written a book called *A Stepladder to Farming*. His son farmed Landway in Jameston but he died tragically young, and Robert Halliday's son Jack took the farm over, and continued the 'early' market until he retired.

Their lorry drivers, Brian Eldred and Dennis Hancock, lived at what was then called Lower Bubbleton, now Giltar Grove.

Dennis Hancock later practised market gardening at Swallow Tree in Saundersfoot, and his son John, now runs the very successful Swallow Tree Holiday Complex.

In 1938 the telephone kiosk outside the post office was to be lit with electricity, it would not be lit very long, the second World War was about to begin.

The village school had maintained a fine standard of ability and a good reputation, but now there was to be an added excitement. Over the two years 1940-1 there was an intake of 49 evacuees from all over the country. Many of these children were relatives of their hosts, but others were from large cities with no rural experience, and they found life strange indeed. Judging by the School Attendance Records, all of these evacuees returned home within a year, perhaps that is why few are remembered.

Remnants of the air-raid shelter can still be seen in the playground. It was during the War that all schoolchildren benefited by having a free half pint of milk every morning, and a hot midday meal for a small amount of money.

The great stalwart Hugh Angell died in 1940, and the parish council was in a dilemma as to whether he needed to be replaced as a Trustee of the Cooke Charity. A death certificate was needed to send to Bryant & May, the matchmakers, to 'strike' his name.

Preparations against a possible invasion by the enemy were underway at this time, and the South beach was staked and obstructed. Concertina barbed wire and land mines covered the dunes, and accounted for at least one death when tragically someone was blown up. Laurie Evans of Court Farm helped to retrieve the remains.

Meanwhile the villagers enthusiastically took up allotments on offer in order to supplement their diet, and they could make application to keep a pig.

Those in the reserved occupation of farming spent their war years growing whatever the country needed, and on demand. Hitherto unknown crops like flax and anything that would relieve the risks to our Merchant Fleet. Land Army girls replaced the men that had gone to fight, and later, Italian and German prisoners were used too.

The Local Defence Volunteers were formed which soon became the Home Guard, but there was bitter disappointement when keen young farmers found themselves in a 'reserved' occupation.

The Penally Home Guard platoon was made up with men from New Hedges. Fortunately, Wyn Phillips (2nd row, see photograph page 146) was able to remember nearly all the men in the next picture which was taken behind the old village hut.

It was first erected in 1922, and replaced with a more solid structure

62 years later, but the original had served the community well and seen many village 'hops' and celebrations, often organised by Wyn's father, Jack Phillips.

No. 2 Platoon Penally H.G. (Vernon Evans collection).

Back row: Stanley Davies. Fred Williams. Albert Williams. Ted Morton. Tommy Stevens and Derek Williams.
2nd row: ?. Fred Morgan. Gil Roberts. ?. Levi Thomas. Austin Nash. Wyn Phillips and Colwyn Phillips (brothers).
3rd row: Tommy Morgan. Cyril Cavill. Archie Edwards. ? Harris. Vernon Evans. John Meyrick. Billy Lawrence. Arthur Hughes. Tom Williams.
Seated: Cpl. Eric Haines. Cpl. Tommy Richards. Sgt. Tom Morton. Jack Phillips. Lt. H. Howells (pop). Captain A. Wheeler. Lt. Ashley Colley.
5th row: Cpl. Billy Harris. Davies the Bank. Lomax Black Rock Café. Saunders. Freddie Brace. Dennis Hancock. Wallace Buttland. ? Neal.

At the beginning of the War, Laurie Evans had moved his family, along with all his stock and implements from Kilawen Farm in Saundersfoot to Bubbleton. A tremendous undertaking in wartime with no transport or petrol available, only carts.

Dr Mathias bought Court Farm in 1941 and immediately offered it to

Laurie, which meant another move. His son Vernon bought Bubbleton later, and his grandson Martin, is now one of the few still farming.

Court Farm had a German prisoner of war from 1945-8 named Alois Feldbauer from Pfatter in Regensburg, and to this day, the two families have kept in touch.

An amusing story Vernon told me concerned Loftus Phillips who lived at Lydstep during the war, and had not long married a Miss Meyrick. Loftus was a soldier at the time and decided to absent without leave to see his new wife. Penally Police Constable Griffiths was sent to arrest him. You can imagine the comedy of seeing Loftus being led through the village on his way to Tenby station behind a bicycle.

The history of the constabulary having a presence in the village started with Benjamin Evans in the 1880's who lived with his Irish wife Ellen at 2 The Commons. He was followed by Tom Nash before the first World War and then there was William Pike through the 1930's, followed by William McTaggart just before the last War.

Henry Griffiths was the last policeman to live at Raymond House which was traditionally the police station for Penally, and finally, Reg Scales, a Yorkshire man who had a house built for him at Lydstep, ended the period of the 'local bobby'.

Court Farm was used as a staging post for cattle from Caldey island right up until the years after World War 2. The monks swam them over the dangerous stretch of water at the right tide and in calm conditions, towed by ropes. The currents were such that it meant first going in one direction and then another, and there was always the danger of a beast getting caught up in the rope.

Brother Thomas, a large man and much loved character in the area, would often jump into the water to help the cattle untangle their legs. It must have been a hazardous business, but eventually they were housed in sheds at Court until they were transported to market.

Sir David Hughes-Morgan Bart: died in March 1941 aged 70. He had been High Sheriff of Brecon, J.P. and eight times Mayor of Tenby.

Allotments were in a disgusting state of neglect by 1942 according to parish councillor Dr Charlie, only three were cultivated. It was not long after this that they were abandoned. The reason was probably that few men remained to tend them.

The War took another turn in 1943 when 'Exercise Jantzen' got underway. It was part of the preparation for our invasion of the enemy called OVERLORD. Penally camp was used to train troops for these D Day landings. It has been said that Winston Churchill viewed the execises from Wiseman's Bridge.

An Avro Anson I of No. 217 Squadron over the Pembrokeshire Coast at Tenby — seven of this type were based at Carew Cheriton in June, 1939. But with its restricted bomb load and no detection equipment the Anson was little improvement on the aircraft which had operated from there in World War One.
(Picture, Imperial War Museum)

This photograph was used as a poster by the Government. One can recognise Penally below the plane, even though the aerial view tends to flatten out the Ridgeway.

The American soldiers based at Penally drove hundreds of tons of stone from the quarry opposite the camp. Endless lorry loads drove through the village during the months of July and August to make the runway required at Wiseman's Bridge. No doubt they created a little dust and noise. At that time the camp was an American Field Hospital including 150 nurses.

All these preparations for landing rehearsals meant that restrictions were imposed on any movement of civilians up to 6 miles inland, and special passes were reqired to get into different areas. There was also a curfew.

Billy Roberts, the plumber, remembers Eric Haines, the cobbler, being strafed by a lone German plane when he was on Giltar cliffs, and that an unexploded bomb fell on Baldwins Moor.

A chap known to all as Hong Kong Charlie from Tenby, claimed that his father on anti-submarine patrol on the cliffs, had disabled a U Boat and that oil was seen to rise to the surface!

In December 1944 the Home Guard stood down.

Because of hostilities the village had remained static in the matter of new house building. There were approximately 100 houses from Bower Cottages to Holloway, they numbered only 45 more than there were in 1890.

After the War ended a Welcome Home Fund for returning service men inspired a flat horse race over ½ a mile circuit, to be run at Trefloyne and organised by Jack Phillips, who lived there. It was also hoped that profits might help towards replacing the old village hall.

These races happened over four or five meetings but good prize money had to be offered to attract the best riders and horses, and sadly there was not sufficient profit made and the races discontinued.

On one occasion Laurie Evans insisted his youngest son, 6 year old Lloyd, should compete though the child was not very happy. The horse, called Nimble Dick, bolted, but young Lloyd hung on and won the race.

The parish council was concerned about the road leading to the beach which had been badly cut up by the overuse of Army lorries. It was 1946, and a letter was sent asking the War Department to restore public access again.

The school building did not get any attention until years after the war, but then many improvements took place under Miss Rotter's guidance. She remained Headmistress for 21 years and was much respected.

In 1948 Jo Morley Joseph had moved into Giltar Grove and taken over from Louis Thomas, the author/farmer. Both Jo and his wife Molly contributed greatly to village affairs through the church and W.I. activities.

The following year a cement project at Lydstep was applied for, at a proposed cost of £1, 500, 000 to employ 600 men. The location was to be west of Whitewell each side of the railway extending to Lydstep Halt.

It was visualised the limestone quarrying would produce half a million tons of cement to be shipped out from Pembroke Dock.

It would cover 500 acres of the best farming land in what was soon to become the Pembrokeshire Coast National Park. The applicaton got planning consent in July 1949, 17 votes for, 9 against.

Letters of protest flooded in from J. Joseph of Giltar Grove, Tenby Town Council, Tenby Hoteliers and residents.

Councillor H. D. Howells of Penally was in favour of the project saying 'South Pembs is a county that lives for 3 months from the crowd and 9 months on each others backs' loud laughter, he added 'that's a fact'. But the howls of protest won the day and it did not go ahead. Although the National Park was not established until 1952, the intent was there and it may have proved a barrier to such applications.

H. V. Thomas from London bought the Lydstep Estate shortly afterwards and the Pembrokeshire Farmers Club was set up in the big house.

The members saw the potential of the long drive down to the house, the beautiful setting and facilities, and with the consent of the owner and led by Owen Davies of Pembroke, they founded a Speed Hill Climb in the autumn of 1949.

It was considered one of the best of its kind in the country and attracted the very best drivers to compete. World Champions like Ken Wharton, and Jack Moore, and commentators like Murray Austin supported races that were run at Easter and September and drew enormous numbers of spectators. These meetings were very exciting and no doubt would have continued but for the development of the Caravan Park.

Still in 1949, Petty Officer G. D. Cavill was presented with an inscribed silver cigarette case by members of the Royal Navy Old Comrades Association. He had taken part in the daring escape of *H.M.S. Amethyst* down the Yangtse river.

Some years later it was felt that a suitable stone that could serve as a memorial for a Cenotaph in the village was needed. One was found near St Deinol's ruins behind the Abbey. The spot where it had stood was called 'Parsons field' and three enthusiasts set themselves the task of transporting it to the place where it now stands on the green.

They were Jo Joseph, Arthur Leather, and Bill Davies, and they used Jo's landrover and a sledge. It was a Herculean effort!

Now there is a move to make a hard-standing for the comfort of the congregation on Armistice Day, led by John Bevan and encouraged by the newly formed Community Association.

The Roll of Honour reads:

In grateful memory of those who gave their lives for their Country

1914-18 Charles Evans; Wlliam John; George Ernest Rees; John Jenkins; H. Berkeley Beynon; William John Williams.
1939-45 James W. Douglas Armstrong; Edmund D. James; Edward George Vare; William J. Stubbs; Charles G. Smith; Ellis Skyrme.

We will remember them

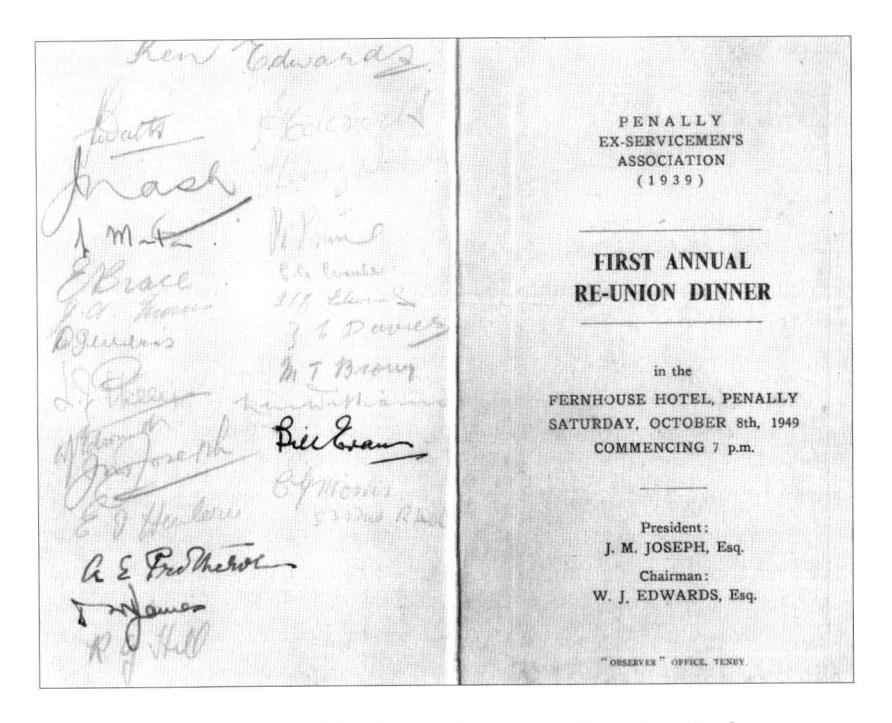

PENALLY
EX-SERVICEMEN'S
ASSOCIATION
(1939)

FIRST ANNUAL
RE-UNION DINNER

in the
FERNHOUSE HOTEL, PENALLY
SATURDAY, OCTOBER 8th, 1949
COMMENCING 7 p.m.

President:
J. M. JOSEPH, Esq.
Chairman:
W. J. EDWARDS, Esq.

"OBSERVER" OFFICE, TENBY.

The menu was pretty bland, but food was still rationed of course, so the company would have been well pleased with white onion soup followed by roast beef and vegetables and fruit tart with custard or trifle and coffee.

Farming at this time was still full of promise, and the early potato crop gave employment to many in the village. However, 'earlies' were never properly marketed, and although there were good years, the crop eventually lost out through the vagaries of the weather, market distances and Egyptian and Jersey imports.

Following the pioneers, the two people to receive the most accolades for their crops over the many years, were Jo Joseph and Vernon Evans farming the two Bubbleton's, pictured left. Specialised planting and harvesting machinery evolved like the 'swipe' which was invented by the previous owner of Crackwell, Colin Mason. Improvements continued, and production advanced until 1974 when farming started to be overshadowed as the main economic backbone of the County, and tourism took over.

The land lying between Lydstep and Crackwell was often referred to as 'the garden of Pembrokeshire' by other farmers in the County.

In 1952 King George VI died, and we moved seamlessly into another Elizabethan reign. It was a time of great expectation, and people were eager to put the past behind them. There were still building restrictions and food rationing, but gradually there was relief from these constraints, and a change in attitudes and values that was to gather momentum.

1953 was the year of the Coronation and a boom in the sales of the new-fangled television. The village hall acquired a set so that everyone in the village could enjoy the historical event for the first time.

Until the new hall was built, voting for all elections took place in the schoolroom. Although it is out of my time brief I have included this last picture of Penally pupils (page 153) because many of these children are still living in the village. They will remember Miss Rotter who set aside time for the children to learn gardening.

Class of 1957.

Back row: Miss Rotter. Roger Evans. David Saunders. Richard Howell. Jennifer Teesdale. Janet Keane. Peter Winstone. Michael Williams. Michael Davies. Brian Daniel. Ann Thomas. Helen Phillips. David Phillips. Mrs Thomas & Mrs Lewis.
Middle row: Phillip James. Ashley Thomas. David Howells. Peter Russell. Ivor Mayhew. Sheila Harrison. Kathleen James. Wendy James. Corin Thompson. Hazel Jenkins. Eleanor Davies. Michael Keane.
Front row: Malcolm Brace. Elliot Phillips. Richard Evans. David Harrison. John Keane. Michael King. Mary James. Linda Morris. Cathy Shannon. Jaqueline Williams. Isabel ?. Gloria Vaughan.

These children and their families will know of the last 50 years of life in Penally before the turn of the century. They will have witnessed the most complete change in the village seen as a community:

The great electricity employer, SWEB, has waxed and waned.
The early potato crop has boomed and bust, and farming is in crisis.
The rail station is now a 'halt', the bustle long over.
The garage closed.
The chapel closed.
The new by-pass once more isolates the village.

Strong characters like Clement Williams, Saurin, Mathias, Voyle and Angell, have not been replaced, but equally, charity and patronage are no longer required or appreciated.

The door has quietly shut on this way of life, and it will fast become a curiosity. We are all able to live more insular lives with less dependence on each other brought about by easy communication through the car, the mobile phone, and the network bringing instant world wide contact.

To end this history, if I had to describe the village today, I would say it is far prettier, more colourful and cared-for than it ever was. There is a pride in its appearance. With the formation of the Community Association, there is now a platform for all residents to make a difference. Hopefully, it will serve the needs of the 21st century.

St Nicholas 1805 by John Norris (note the cross, now removed).

Appendix

An 'Old Crow' who was born in Penally about 1877 submitted the fascinating newspaper cuttings that follow but he lived most of his life in London. I believe his surname was Morgan. (See note at the end of this article).

EIGHTY YEARS OF LIFE AT PENALLY
By
'Old Crow'

Imagine my horror to hear from a noted Welshman that Penally should really be pronounced 'Pennallty'. Such things are not possible.

If one could draw a circle around Tenby, Penally and Manorbier, and right down to Pembroke Dock, I think one would find very little Welsh spoken, if any, by those born and bred in that part of Pembrokeshire.

Penally! Let's go back nearly eighty years when the village was a mere handful of houses. Then it was possible to walk down from 'Starvation' and into Tenby shopping – walking through fields all the time.

And wasn't there excitement when the station was to be built! The old P. and T. Railway Company had many debates as to where it should actually stand. Some wanted it below the 'Commons' others below where Court is now. The latter at that time was a small cottage farm. Anyhow, they fixed the place and built Penally around it where 'Court Lodge' now stands. John Francis had a cottage and the most wonderful tulips, beds of them. In my memory I see them now, gorgeous colourings, in fact, every cottage had glorious flowerbeds.

Do you remember the flowers in the garden where the chapel now stands?

At that time our church was very neglected, grass growing high. The Parson of that time turned his cattle in there over the low wall to eat and destroy at their will. The school was then where the Reading room is now. There were three steps leading down into it. I think

155

there were ten of us. Education was a luxury; even our schoolmaster couldn't give his whole day to it. He taught in the morning and carried the post in the afternoon. He always wore a chimney-pot hat in school – and out! He used to sit close to the fire, a long pointer in his hand, hat tilted over his eyes, the class in a circle around him.

We used to be given a portion of the Bible to read. Woe betide the one who stopped suddenly; it woke him from his nap and down came the pointer with a thud.

Time passed, and our school was moved to the Castle Hill in Tenby, and so we became part of that town. Because of this bond, right through the generations, one finds Tenby and Penally people closely linked. We would like to be one big family, only we don't like your rates.

How many remember the church when our only music was Ben Edwards pitching the hymns starting note on the flute, and then joining in with his rich voice. When the late Rev. D. M. Morris came to our village, bringing young ideas, he put new life into the church and village. The church walls were raised, graves restored, and the church itself renovated.

Miss Clifton herself undertaking the task of beautifying the churchyard, she planted flowers everywhere until our little churchyard, especially at Easter-time was a beautiful sight. People were encouraged to pay attention to graves; bulbs could always be had from Miss Clifton for the asking.

Then the late Mr and Mrs Clement Williams took a great interest in the church. They installed electric light throughout the church, the cost and upkeep being generously borne by that gentleman. Later he gave the organ, and I believe the bells. His death was a great loss to the village. He loved all children and animals. I remember Mrs C. Williams having little earthenware saucers fixed along the paths in the grounds at the back of the 'House', which the cowman filled with milk every morning for all the cats to feed from.

I think some of the finest pigeons in the country had their home over the stables there. Every year he had his workmen fix a huge swing on the trees just below the Abbey, for the benefit of the village children. He had the room above the church fixed up as a reading room for the men of the village, and billiard and bagatelle tables were fixed – even football and cricket equipment for the men and the boys.

Article 2

Every year there was a tea in the grounds for the children, a big field at the back being turned into a pleasure ground for races, rounders, etc. Mr William's himself would always have the first innings of rounders, and my word, couldn't he send the ball away! A wonderful day ended with a procession past them, and to receive from Mrs Clement William's own hands an orange, a bag of sweets and a new penny.

In those days every 'Big House' had its stables and coachmen and some fine turnouts there were. I think the 'Big House' came first with Davies on the box and George, the footman beside him. Those horses and carriages were a sight for sore eyes. The Vicarage second, with Cavanagh on the box, third Mrs Voyle, with Barson on the box, then Mrs Mathias, with Davy Davies as coachman, and the 'Mount' with Jim Griffiths.

Those were great old days. There were not so many distractions for the young people. Yearly events were things one looked forward to, and talked of all the year. The different gentry gave a Christmas tree and tea in the school, followed by dancing and games. Those were the days of energetic polkas and dreamy waltzes. The little ones had their pleasure until seven, the grown-ups from seven to ten.

I have a happy memory of a portly gentleman leading the 'Bobby Bingo' song with a voice that I am sure reached Tenby, and couldn't he 'shake a leg'! To see him and partner dance the polka was like a present day vision of Kaye Don trying a new record. He was the idol of those happy gatherings; nothing was complete if he wasn't in it.

Then there was Sanger's Circus, a yearly event that everyone went to see in Tenby; and Poole's Myriorama, more often called Poole's Myarama. No one thought of queues then, everyone pushed to the door, the stronger ones got in first. How we loved those moving pictures, and the conductor and his long stick who took us on 'a trip around the world'.

I have heard many old Penallyites debate, which was the nicer, Easter at home, or Christmas. Easter with its flowers and country beauty, or Christmas with its village pleasures. I am speaking of bygone days. The walks over the Burrows. Through Trefloyne woods, over the Ridgeway, down Whitewell and round by Bubbleton to the village were wonderful at Easter time. The view from the Ridgeway looking over Tenby is like looking at a rare jewel. Later in summertime to wander over the glorious sands and up to Giltar for a Sunday evening to sit on Black Rock and hear the bells of St Mary's – heavenly music, giving us hope of a better life to come.

An American visitor who, hearing me praise Tenby and Penally had a short holiday there, said, "your little town and our way of advertising, and your shopkeepers would be millionaires in six months." He may be right, but it then would be like Blackpool, etc. I am all in for developments, and would like to see our villages everywhere improved in modern conveniences and labour saving devices installed. They want telephones, decent roads, proper drainage, electric light or gas. Years ago when anyone was ill, a man would have to go off on a bicycle or walk to the nearest doctor. A public telephone box would help that sort of thing. By all means teach charabanc trippers decorum and do all that we can to keep and make the countryside beautiful but it is development, not preservation that the countryside needs.

Tenby doesn't advertise itself half enough. I have been in cinemas in our large towns where beauty spots in North Wales are thrown up on the screen, but never Tenby!

Pass on to Christmas-time at home. Here let me mention Tenby resembles Ireland in its use of 'sobriquets' But let it not be supposed that the nicknames are given in a spirit of unkindness- far from it. The person who excites it may as frequently be the object of sympathy as of mirth and many of the people I might name, I never knew their proper names and no offence is meant.

Article 3

Take for instance the gang of railway men whose Christian names were all William. There had to be a difference.

At Christmas-time we had the 'Waits' who regularly started their music at captain Pascoe's at Court Lodge – the fiddles, the cello, a few brass instruments and I believe a banjo. I only knew their nickname. We liked their coming because it meant the boys of the village would be home soon from the Army and Navy. There are very few houses in Penally where one, if not more of the family have spent some years abroad.

The Servants Balls at Christmas time were wonderful affairs, usually coming after the tea and tree in the schoolroom. The Haven gave several good ones in the late Lady Nora Phillips' time, also amateur theatricals, where all the young people of the leading houses performed. The great affair was the 'Abbey Ball' in Mr and Mrs T. D. Cunningham's time.

It was a gorgeous affair. There was a large staff of servants and all were allowed to invite several friends. The butler and lady's maid spared no effort to make it a success. Mr Cunningham was, if I remember rightly, the first to bring motor cars to the village.

Then there was the concert in the school, which Miss Clifton and Miss Pullen got up annually, a very happy affair. I have an old programme by me as I write. It recalls happy memories.

Who could sing 'White Wings' like T.E. or 'Little Brown Jug' like T.B. or 'Uncle Ned' like T.M. or 'Cockles and Mussels, Alive Alive' like H.O. or 'We'll all go home to roost' like the gardener at Colonel Goodeve's and Mr Hugh Griffiths, Trefloyne, singing 'D'ye ken John Peel' and Mr Dick Williams of Tenby, singing, 'I'm off to Philadelphia in the morning' and Ben Edwards singing 'The Ivy Green'.

At these events our late beloved Vicar, the Rev. D. M. Morris, always honoured us with his presence. I think he was a great Christian man, broadminded, and an aristocrat to his fingertips.

In those days the soldiers from the Barracks were made to feel quite at home, and worshipped at the same time as the villagers. He was a Chaplain of the Forces, and loved soldiers. Any village girl marrying a soldier was always given the wedding fee as her first wages. Since his death I visited the church, and as I went near the altar, I felt as if he was in the church. I missed all the chairs near the altar where the soldiers here always sat for years.

Is there any other church which has the funny side places for sitting. Or built in the shape of a 'T'? Many years ago it was believed that there was an underground passage from the Abbey. Where the old ruins now are, leading into the church, and that there was a place in the roof where a monk slept.

We can't pass Christmas without the New Year's Concert. The programme beside me gives names of many who lost their lives in the Great War, and of a young nurse who died of fever at a very early age, but let's go back many years when Penally didn't have a chapel.

The late Mr J. M. Griffiths came to the village, lodged there, and watched the Court being enlarged to his own requirements. He was the last of that great class, 'The gentleman farmers'.

He was a great Chistian and was greatly worried because the village had no chapel. To meet this he gave the use of his large clean barn for religious services. He laboured many years until the present chapel was built.

I think the names of all those who collected with the coins and papers of that year were put in the corner stone of the chapel.

The late Mr Cocker of Tenby, was a great friend of Mr Griffiths and gave many a helping hand to the chapel, also Mr F. Craven of Bradford who gave the old silver, communion service, two-handled cups, etc. which have now been replaced by glasses.

The large family at 'Court' gave their services freely to the chapel. Miss Elizabeth for many years played the harmonium, which was later replaced with an organ. Mr Griffith had a fine bass voice, and was a good musician.

Article 4

We were all very proud of Miss Mary when she was appointed to Queen Victoria's service, and everyone in the village was allowed to see the presents which the Royal Family gave her when she left and had to come home to manage the housekeeping owing to the ill-health of her mother. Later she was lecturing and could speak well on anything concerned with the dairy.

One's heart is saddened to read the names of so many of that family who lie buried abroad. They are fondly remembered in the village. Many old 'crows' with whom I have spoken say how the religious training they had in the Congregational Sunday School has helped them. Some of the old Sunday school hymns were a great help, especially Nos. 117, 62, 127, 306 in Sankey and Moody. There have been some good old Christian preaching. There was one whose only name I ever knew was 'Spurgeon'. He would preach in a small voice and tell of the wages of sin, etc., then suddenly preach in a voice of thunder, awaking the soundest sleeper. I believe our favourite preacher was Mr Nicholls, a Tenby tailor. He never preached at you. He gave out the text and then leaned on the pulpit and had a heart-to- heart talk with you and one was made to feel that by not being a Christian, it was our great loss.

Let us go with a younger generation to the school. Its examination. Mrs Osborne has coached them all well, the school is freshly scrubbed, children dressed with care. Mr Bancroft, the Inspector, can be seen walking leisurely over the fields from Tenby. How many dreaded that day?

I read in the *Tenby Observer* recently that village boys were not well behaved. Well, a generation or so back, mischievous deeds were rife, and by some of the older generation, who unfortunately forget their own youth. An old busybody once couldn't resist putting the then young boys in their places; he was promptly trussed up and put under the table whilst they finished their games. Another 'young blood' now an old gentleman, who attained high rank in the Army, during a tea party on the Burrows to commemorate Queen Victoria's Jubilee, put salt in the huge cans of tea, instead of sugar!

One thing Penally has lost, and that is the village green as a playground for village children. Grass, weeds and brambles are allowed to grow waist high, it is nobody's property, so nobody looks after it. The middle green will soon be a huge cinder path. The second green, or 'Palace Garden' as it used to be called, is now I believe private property and children are nor allowed to play on it. Roads in these days are dangerous, the Burrows is out of the question because of the distance for young children. I should like to have seen these greens laid out as playing fields for rounders, etc. for the younger children, the further one could be wired in. If this had been done as a memorial to all those gallant village boys who fought for their country and to those who lost their lives in the Great War, it would have been better than all the tablets.

Another thing which should be altered is the objectionable habit people have, who after cleaning their graves, put all the refuse as near the gate (by the Palace Garden) as possible. There should be a sunken pit where this could be burnt or buried; and some of the tombstones of those who have left the village for years, want 'Pennallty' indeed! No, Penally, place of happy memories.

* * *

The only Morgan family I could find in the village in 1877 was that of John and Rebecca Morgan, Stone Mason with five children. The house was not named, but it was next door to Rock Villa. One of the sons was Henry aged 4. Could this be 'Old Crow'?

In 1989 A few taped recordings of people in the village were made by Mary Smith, for the W.I. project that year. Here are the transcriptions.

Mansell Brown, who was born in 1902, lived at 'Alma' with his uncle Tom Brown who farmed New House just at the back of them. Mansell's father was a haulage contractor for the Army Camp, with horses and wagons. There were two goods trains every day. When he went to school he remembered only the Vicarage and what was Railway Cottage, being the only houses nearby. He wore corduroy trousers to school and he walked to Tenby to have his hair cut at Abbey Morse's – 'too far to walk now,' he added (he was 87 years old at this interview).

He attended Church three times on Sunday, at 11 a.m., Sunday School at 2.30 and again at 6 p.m. The Sunday School treat was a trip to Saundersfoot with the horse and wagon all polished up, and the small children in a gambo.

He left school at the age of 13; his mother wanted his voice trained. After service in WW2, he worked at the Army Camp for 22 years.

Maisie Brown, born Maisie Morgan at Whitehouse next to the Cross Inn.

There were 24 people in 2 families of 12 each. Her father worked on farms and then became a linesman with the railway. She was church caretaker for 21 years.

She remembered Mr Owens used to deliver paraffin, and Mr Handley from Tenby, 'stuck' the pig. They also kept bantams and chickens. She picked herbs and flowers on the burrows during the War for medicines. Gramophone records were played in the village hall on social evenings, Jack Phllips ran them, and there were sixpenny hops on Thursday nights.

On her views of the village today she thought it could not be called a village today. She remembered that the village, known as 'the commons' used to stretch from the side of the camp to Mollie Whitehead's house.

She considered the by-pass a mixed blessing, and golf, a threat to life.

Doris Kemp, wife of the Tenby Chiropodist, was born Doris Morgan of 'Hillcrest'.

She described her grandfather, Tom Morgan, as dogsbody for the church; he dug graves, rang bells, and did wood carving. Mrs Kemp wore mutton boots to school, only the wealthy wore shoes. She enjoyed going to Miss James' village shop it was a great place for a chat. She remembered there was always a maypole on May Day and parties for the children were plentiful. The Saurins gave all, gifts at Christmas, fruit and sweets for the children, soap and hankies for the adults.

In her view the village is ruined and over-developed, she was especially grieved that Strawberry Gardens' lovely wall was destroyed.

Leslie Edwards of Rock Villa was born in that house, he was one of five children, and Albert, his father, was the postman. His grandfather Thomas was a tailor. His great grandfather, Benjamin, was also born in the village in 1823, a quarry man at Black Rock. Thus the family can be traced back for at least 200 years and Leslie must be the oldest surviving member of this original Penally family. Leslie is rather reticent, but he has been invaluable as a source of reference, and is an avid collector of village memorabilia.

Gwen Leather founded Penally W.I. in 1953. Her maiden name was Haines and she was born in 1918 at Picton Cottage. One of eight children, she went to the village school and remembered there were about 50 other children, some from Lydstep, and Whitewell who walked all the way every day, each with a bottle of tea. She had music lessons in Tenby and walked there with Dick Tasker the Postman. Johnny Raines delivered bread to the village until Mr Brown set up at a ½ penny cheaper. There were dances at the Village Hall run by Harold Howells and Captain Angell, but there was not much social life as such. Funerals were more interesting.

Tom Tipton was the butler at Penally House and Nurse John the midwife from Lydstep.

In 1999, just days before she died, she talked further with my colleague Ruth Griffiths, and here are notes from that conversation.

Sunday School Outing – 65 years ago. She and Ann Molten were given a book, which was signed by the churchwardens and told to collect for the outing. They always started with Mrs Gibbon in Heywood Lane because if she gave 5/- the Saurins wouldn't like to give less. The trip was usually to Haverforwest and Milford, and the big point of it all was to visit Woolworth's! There wasn't one in Tenby and it was considered wonderful, One year, the church ladies from Milford forgot to organise the tea, which they had promised, so Ann and Gwen did it. Captain Angell was so impressed with their efforts that he took them to Woolworth's and bought them a carrier bag of goodies each and then gave them a ride home in his car, while everyone else went on the 'chara'. The Christmas party was held in the church room and paid for by Major Saurin.

Sir David Hughes Morgan provided the tree. When Major Saurin came down at the end of the party, all the children sang 'for he's a jolly good fellow'.

She recalled Miss Clifton of Clifton Cottage, and her bright ginger wig. On Maundy Thursday the entire village turned out to pick primroses that then had to be tied in bunches of 12, with wool but no leaves. The flowers were delivered at Clifton Cottage whereupon the maid took them and stood them in bowls of water and the children were allowed to play in the garden for ½ hour exactly.

They were then given a hot-cross bun and a cream egg each. The primroses were used to decorate the church on Saturday morning, and on the window facing the door the word 'Hallelujah' was made in primroses. Miss Clifton also organised a Christmas concert in the school.

The Abbey employed a big staff in the Saurin's time, including 3 gardeners, as the gardens were then also on the lower side of the road with tennis courts where there is now a bungalow. They entertained a lot and had huge tennis parties. They had a butler, housemaid, parlourmaid, ladies maid Lizzie Ridge and a cook and an undercook.

'The Plots' (allotments) rent was 3/6 per annum and it was a popular evening walk to visit the plots and inspect other peoples veg: Messrs Morgan, Williams, James, Edwards, Nash, Haines, and Phillips are the remembered gardeners

Gorse Cottage was just two rooms occupied by Mr and Mrs Gardner. They had family in Pontypridd, so may not have been local. They were caretakers of the chapel for which they were paid 1/- a week. Mrs Gardner used to provide lunch on Sunday for the preacher which was always 'a little bit of meat with veg: they'd grown themselves' and as a Sunday treat, an enamel bowl of rice pudding.

The chapel was spotless and all the oil lamps 'in good trim'. They had one son Tommy who left Penally. Mr Gardner was also a postman. They had folding beds and a 'skew' and a big smoky fire which they use to 'ball' every morning. The balls were made from culm, which they bought from Bonvilles Court, and clay, which they fetched in a handcart from Drussleton.

When asked her views of Penally today, she thought progress was necessary, but did not want the village to get any bigger.

Gwen Haines passed the scholarship to Tenby Grammar School along with her chums Mary Rees and Ann Morton. She later married Arthur Leather, the manager of Melias in Tenby where she worked.

Interviewed in 1999 by M. Davies:
Renee Wall, née Williams, born 1920 at Banjeston, of long established farming families of Tarr, Carswell and Roberts Wall. She had a wartime marriage to Frank Wall who was born at Redhouse in New Hedges.

The Crown Inn, Penally, belonged to Frank's father, and she ran the pub for a few years whilst Frank was working for the Agriculture Department during the War.

She remembered Reuben Lewis, an ex Royal Navy man, who acted as a sort of guardian to young Renee in the pub whilst Frank was away. Reuben was on a pension that he could not help spending badly, so Renee looked after his money for him. One day he asked for some money to buy three shirts and returned later, tipsy, but with all three shirts under the one he was wearing. However, Reuben was useful dealing with the many rough soldiers in the bar.

Of the local characters, she recalled blind young D. F. Thomas regularly walking over from Trefloyne to the pub with his greyhounds, and remembered Dr Charlie well. When she showed the doctor upstairs to her grandmother's bedroom he remarked that she was a 'long legged bloody animal'.

She met Heather Angel, the actress, many times when she called at the pub.

* * *

Mr Thomas is a 61 year old, former electrical engineer, who lives at Pixie Grove in Penally, has been water diving for 20 years.

He walked several miles in order to trace supplies on Caldey.

"For the contractors it would have been hit or miss," he said. "I pointed out where to drill, and they were able to find the water 60ft below the surface. It was a pleasure to be able to help the monks."

The monks, who are pledged to poverty, faced a bill of £300 a day for engineers and a drilling rig from Tenby.

An Island spokesman, Father Stephen, said, "Mr Thomas was quite impressive with his methods. He even found a water pipe buried inches below concrete in our farmyard."

From newspaper report and audio tape done by BBC 1974.

*   *   *

Reminiscences of Old Penally by Miss May Beynon
From Editor's Postbag
Weekly Observer
Friday, Aug. 12th, 1960

I remember quite well Mr Clement Williams, who drove his carriage and pair to Tenby most days. He often gave my brother and me a lift inside his closed carriage (open in summer) on our way from school, thus giving us the thrill of a lifetime and a feeling that we had suddenly become King and Queen of England. I don't think Mr Williams would have felt so kindly disposed to us had he known we often ran behind his carriage and hoisted ourselves on the bar at the back, which gave us a glorious ride behind the prancing horses, but we were not able to hop off until speed was slowed down on approaching a hill.

Then there were Mr and Mrs Cunningham, The Abbey, to whom I supplied three pennyworth of milk every morning on my bicycle before school, keeping the account myself, and every month I asked Miss Beddoes of the Post Office, to enter the cash on my Post Office book.

I well remember Mrs Donoghoe who, I believe, still resides in Penally and is a great age. She once made a costume for me better than any tailor.

Any excuse was made for a visit to the village from Holloway Farm, and I loved spending my Saturday halfpenny with Miss James at the Shop.

I believe 'Old Crow' in a former letter mentioned Willie Hendy, who played ball games on Penally Green with the village boys. He was my cousin and lived for some years with my family at Holloway Farm. He died in New Zealand about five years ago, aged 78.

Last, but by no means least, was the lovely, happy, hard-working Mrs Kitty Gough (not Miss) whom 'old crow' describes so aptly and truly. She (and Dr Hamilton) brought my brother into the world and every Monday came to us at 8 a.m. for a full day's washing and was paid only 1/- and her dinner.

What a dear good woman she was, always smiling, joking and often bouncing us up and down on her tired knees, which was loved. To walk to her cottage was a joy – up the rugged narrow pathway through the enchanting Hoyle woods, which in spring would be aglow with primroses, violets (white and blue), anemones and ferns, plus the liquid notes of bird song, a veritable fairy land.

Above this wood one came to an open field, in which her cottage was situated. She would usually spot a visitor approaching across the field and wait in the doorway with her welcoming happy smile. The cottage was a very old two-roomed one with a thatched roof.

What a joy it was to be invited inside and sit by the huge fire. She once told me of a snake that fell from the thatch into the fire! In the little passage dividing the two rooms there stood a dresser crammed with china, great and small, and once before my departure, she presented me with a tiny little jug and I left for home just floating on air. Her son, Tommy Gough, a nice quiet fellow, rented a coach-house in our farmyard for a £1 a year, which he used as a carpenter's shop, and an excellent carpenter he was. He made a beautiful 'gambo' for my father, which was worked for many years and was as good as ever when sold on my father's retirement. Then cupid struck – we had a splendid maid called Jinny, who married Tommy and raised a family.

I remember James Griffiths, of Penally Court, and his father, who was an expert judge of cattle. A niece of James Griffiths was Gladys Thomas, who lived for while at Penally Court, later becoming Mrs Butler. She now lives in London.

*   *   *

From the *Pembrokeshire Times*
A FORGOTTEN LITERARY HOAX. By Arthur Leach. Feb: 19.1930
Number 1 mermade Street
Penally
Siptimbcr forth, 1890
Sur
Wil you Plezc Reed this. there as been found heer a curus box with a ole buk in it it were tuk by me an mi mate bil Winch wile we was trorling orf the Corldy bed it is rote on in ole leters an got pitchers in it they ar ships as wud nevr sale an we carnt tel wot

It is the Skule maister he say as it is verry ole and beelongcd to Culumbuss an is is logg im as dishcovered Merrika butt we dunt nun on us Hold with eddecashun an wee thinx he be larkin but master Garnon thats our Karpenter say as you no all abot them thinks and wil treat its fare i have sent the Think to you by the trane an me an me mate wud bee pertikler obliged if yu wud tel us wot it is, if it is werth anithink pleez send us a triffle for it

I remane

Jonas G. okes.

for Mister Elyacht Stok

Lundun.

One thing remains unexplained. On the cover of the book below the title is this inscription:

S.

S.A.S.,

X.M.Y.

XPoFERENS.Z

Is this another version of: +BILST-UM- PSlII-S-M-ARK?

* * *

The letter by the fisherman 'Okes', of Penally, could certainly not have imposed upon 'any but the half-witted'. A reason for associating the 'discovery' with this district may be found in the fact that Mr Elliot Stock the Publisher about this time was a frequent visitor to Manorbier. The letter, was an obvious joke?

Nearly forty years ago an astonishing prospectus sent out by a reputable firm of publishers, Elliot Stock, of Paternoster Row told how, there came into the hands of several people in Tenby:

Columbus's Log Book
The Alleged Discovery off Tenby

It advertised a forthcoming publication of "The Secrete Log Boke of Christopher Columbus, noted and written by himself in the years 1492-1493." Accompanying this prospectus was a facsimile of an 'original' letter in which two Penally fishermen communicated to Mr Elliot Stock the news of their remarkable discovery of this document, which they claimed to have fished up near Caldey on August 10, 1890. This letter is given below; its false address, suggestive signature, carefully manufactured and incredible miss-spellings, concocted by someone familiar with 'Cockney' errors of speech, but ignorant of the dialectical peculiarities of south Pembrokeshire could have deceived no one in this district.

If a really serious hoax was attempted some very elementary precautions were neglected. Yet some unwary ones were 'bitten', and a copy of the 'Log Boke', bought at second hand many years ago, lies now on my table.

A curious coincidence prompts the writing of this note. The 'Log Boke', after lying undisturbed and quite forgotten in its box for several years, came unexpectedly to light during a search for a pamphlet. The next day a new book on *Enigmas*, by Lt.-Com. R. T. Gould, R.N., came into my hands at a library, and my attention was attracted by a chapter on 'The Land-fall', or first landing-place of Columbus on the American side of the Atlantic.

While reading the discussion of this problem, not with any thought of seeking information about the 'Log Boke', which had quite passed out of my mind, the following sentence brought me to a pause: 'The original journal of Columbus, and the map which he is believed to have drawn to accompany it, are lost – probably irretrievably.' Here, then, might be some light upon the hoax of 1890.

In a footnote, Lieut.-Com. Gould adds: "Some years before the war there were produced in Germany (by Rangette, of Dusseldorf) a number of what were purported to be facsimile reproductions of the lost copy of Columbus' journal, which he is known to have jettisoned" (during a storm off the Azores) when returning to Spain from his first voyage.

It is difficult to believe that they could ever have seriously been intentioned to impose upon any but the half-witted. The text, based on Las Casas, is written in a pseudo-Gothic semi-cursive hand, and in English (in my copy), the reason alleged for this being that Columbus had intentionally kept this 'secret journal' in a foreign tongue.

I believe this hoax was published simultaneously in several countries, the language employed for the text being varied accordingly. The book also contained what purported to be a facsimile of Columbus' commission as; Admiral, and was appropriately bound in brown paper, decorated with sea-shells, pebbles, algae &c.

My copy corresponds exactly with the one described by Lt. Com. Gould, even to the bits of seaweed (or moss) and shells carefully glued on the parchment-paper cover. According to a statement on the cardboard box in which this precious volume was issued it was printed by Franz Rangette and Sons, at Dusseldorf, the London publisher being, as stated above, Elliot Stock Las Casas (mentioned in the above extract from *Enigmas*), the only first-hand authority for the voyage of Columbus, was Bishop Las Casas, who gives in his *Historias dc las Indias*, 1561, some extracts, made possibly from a copy or from the original journal of Columbus.

* * *

The following is taken from 'Pembrokeshire Parsons' p. 241/2 (except for italics by author):

The advowson of Penally Church was, with a perch of land in Penally, granted to the Prioress and Convent of Aconbury by John de Barri of Manorbier, who obtained licence for this purpose from the King on March 1st 1301 – *Pat.Rolls.*

Ann de Barri, the Prioress was the daughter of the Lord of the Manor of Manorbier and Penally.

In 1535-6 the rectory of Penally was leased by the convent of Aconbury-To-Lunteley at the clear yearly rent of £10 13s 4d – *Valor Eccl.*

VICARS

1363	William	Described as 'Sir William, vicar of Penali' he was witness to a conveyance of Land in Penally – *Ancient Deeds Cal.*
1398	John Cook	Collated by the Bishop.

No account for 100 years due to Owain Glyndŵr revolts in Wales and 100 Years War with France.

1502	Lewis Wlliams	
1502	James Rogers	Lewis Williams, deceased.
1503	Galfrid Warburton	
1535-6	William Jenyns	He signed the abjuration of papal authority 1534.
1554	John Griffuts	
1565	David Williams	
1565	Walter Price	David Williams, deceased.
1600	Harry Riley	
1624	Francis Hudson	Turned out of his living in 1650; he is said to have been a pluralist – *Walker's Suff. Clergy.*
?	Ethelred Wogan	His son b. Penally 1678, author of *The Proper Lessons of the Church of England.*
1685	Robert Angel	
1688	Henry Poole	He subscribed to the King's supremacy for Penally and St Florence.
1696	David Rice	
1737	John Williams	David Rice, deceased.
1757	Joseph Hughes	John Williams, deceased.
1764	John Thomas	
1799	Benjamin Gibbon	John Thomas, deceased.
1813	Henry Bevan	Benjamin Gibbon deceased.
1819	John Hughes	Bevan to another living.
1873	David Melvill Morris	He gave the font cover to the church.
1874	E. Lincoln Lewis	
1937	David Davies	
1945	Thomas Morgans	
1952	William Jones	

After the Gunpowder Plot of 1605, laws against Roman Catholics (and curiously, against smokers also) were strictly enforced, and the following ladies were singled out for excommunication:

Alice Tooley, wife of Thomas Bowen of Trefloyne
Bridget Tooley, wife of Thomas Tooley
Katherine Tooley of Arnolds Hill
Mary Tooley, wife of Charles Bowen of Trefloyne.

In 1642 there was a purge of Quakers in the County, better known as the Society of Friends, they had upset the establishment and arrests were made. There is a list of 28 rich burgesses and County families in the Great Sessions that went on trial 'for unlawful meeting, and pretence of religious worship and evil principles in disobedience of his Majesty's Government.'

Many of these families later immigrated to America and continued their faith in Pennsylvania.

In 1656 their founder, George Fox, visited Tenby. A group of local Friends accompanied him and his companion Thomas Holme on their way to Pembroke as far as the waterside. At a point beyond Marsh Farm, where the road dips down to the marsh, they knelt in prayer, before Fox and Holme rode on. I think it unlikely they stopped in Penally, since there was no village centre as such, but they did stop in Jameston, and it was there a Quaker Meeting House was set up opposite what is now the Swanlake Inn.

Finally, in 1689 after a period of eighty year of religious unrest, there was the Toleration Act, and the vicars of Penally follow in ordered pattern.

A Reverend James gave the west door and the altar rail to the church in 1952.

*   *   *

Appendix

OF THE WOR

SUNDAY, JULY 25, 1954

Telephones: Central 3030
Telegrams: Worldly, Fleet.

WHEN NOON IS PAST

THE morning's tasks are over and the workers on Mr. Laurie Evans's farm at Penally, Pembrokeshire, welcome their d-day break. Valerie, the farmer's daughter, ings in Peter, the carthorse, and two race-rses 'Fair Quebec and Arctic Falls, from their paddock. It's a rest, too, for Rummy, the collie, while Shan, the corgi, watches with a superior air from a gatepost. And in the background the church of St. Teilo broods, as it has done down the centuries, over the quiet country scene.

from the Evans' family collection.

Penally was awarded the Lord Merthyr Trophy as the Best-Kept Village in Pembrokeshire in 1962. From left to right: Councillor T. Richards, Vice-Chairman, Pembrokeshire Association of Local Councils, Alderman W. J. Jermain, Chairman, Cllr. T. Fuller Lewis, Lord Merthyr, President, and Dillwyn Miles, Secretary.

Acknowledgements

I have had enormous pleasure writing this account, but any success it may have will be because of the generous help I have received from others.

My co-researcher was Ruth Griffiths of Four Greens, Penally. She worked like a beaver and her enthusiasm and support never waned, and my colleague at the Tenby Historical Society, Kevin Thomas, encouraged me throughout.

Sue Baldwin of Tenby Museum generously lent me her history notes which gave the foundation to my own research, and to the eminent historian R. F. Walker who kindly allowed the use of information from his many articles on the Ritec and the Manorial Courts.

Thomas Lloyd of Freestone Hall lent expertise on people and properties, and Val Cochlin of Tenby Library cured my 'comma-itus' and correcting typographical errors. Dillwyn Miles, the author of over a dozen books on Pembrokeshire and a recognised local historian of distinction, wrote the Preface and checked the authenticity, and Roscoe Howells, another local author of note, gave me practical advice.

Local information came in abundance from Gwladys Evans of Pen Alyn and Vernon and Brenda Evans of Bubbleton Farm, as did many old pictures.

Others who contributed were Jennifer Ball, Michael Brown, George Cavill, Sarah Diment, Leslie Edwards and his sister Christine Powling, Julie French, Joan Grey, Ron Hurlow, Elizabeth King of Tenby Museum, Julie Mathias of Penally School, Sheila Morse, Pat and Wynne Phillips, Clair Rendall, Billy Roberts, John Tipton, Liz Thompson of the Ridgeway Society, Irene Wall, G. and E. Warren, John Watts, and Molly Whitehead.

Lawrenny Newton
Great Pencood
Lawrenny
Lawrenny Hall
Lawrenny Ferry
Quay
Creswell Quay
Cresselly
Burnham Hill
Lanesend
Collins Ford
Market Gate
Middleland
Quarrys
West Williamston
Freestone Hall
Sutton
Limestone Quarrys
Park F.
Harolds F.
Upton Castle
Upton
Snails Pill
Millcombe
Cosheston Mountain
Carew Com
Carew Newton
Norchard
Landurwynet
New Shipping
Caerdeith
Carew Br.
Critchurch
Paskeston
Carew Castle
Pinchaston
Sageston Com.
Cosheston
Mill Park
Ford
Birdslane F.
Sageston
Coachland
Nash
New Inn F.
Dairyhays
Parson F.
Carew
Stapelake
Up. Nash
Poyson
Welson
Flemington Mill
Summerton
Flemington
East Jordaston
Winterhall
Strawberry Hill
T. Gate
Houghton
Windsor F.
Lamphey Park
North Down
Red down
St. Florence
Hays F.
West Jordaston
Castle in Ruins
Hodson Hill
Carew Beacon
Parkwell
Coppybush
The Ridge Way
Lamphey
Manorbeer Newton
Allaston
Sunhill
Clagers
West Hill
Newton Cottage
Rock F.
Hodgeston
Old Mill
Lammaston
Jamestown
Middle Hill
Slade
Lit. Portclew
Lake F.
Portclew
Jason Hall
West Moor
Wind hill
East Moor
Park F.
Tar F.
Freshwater East
Castle
Manorbeer
Mill
Freshwater Bay
Swanslake Bay
Hill F.
E. Trewent
W. Trewent
Manorbeer Bay